Reach for Tomorrow

*Unto him that loved us,
and washed us from our sins
in his own blood. (Rev. 1:5)*

Reach for Tomorrow

by
Verna Searle

Division of Logos International
Plainfield, N.J. 07060

All Scripture references are from the King James Version, unless otherwise noted.

REACH FOR TOMORROW
Copyright © 1980 by Logos International
All rights reserved
Printed in the United States of America
Library of Congress Catalog Number: 80-82694
International Standard Book Number: 0-88270-449-4
Logos International, Plainfield, New Jersey 07060

Contents

Preface
Acknowledgments
1 *Dark Is Not Forever* 1
2 *On My Own* 15
3 *Another Dimension* 37
4 *Working It Out* 51
5 *Beyond Myself* 67
6 *Into the Future—Unafraid* 79
7 *Touching Tomorrow* 91
8 *Morning and Joie de Vivre* 103
Bibliography 127

Preface

Out of a very poignant period in my life I have recorded my feelings and beliefs. I have written a testimony from my personal experience. This is a witness to the power of God as He made it possible for me to reconstruct my life following separation and divorce.

In sharing my experience I pray that others may be helped as they seek to cope with the pain and the loss that accompany divorce. Because I have lived through the crisis, I understand the hurt and heartache. I have felt what it is like to suddenly be alone after twenty-nine years of marriage. I have endured the anguish of despair. I have felt the bereftness of loss. The desolation of abandonment. I have survived the agony of hope seemingly withdrawn. I have sensed my mind clouded and my heart numbed in the bitter experience of rejection.

But beyond the horror and the heartbreak I have found strength. I have discovered that there is hope. I have learned that the limitless resources of

God are always available. They are at hand. To be used. Appropriated.

I have recorded my feelings and fears, and faced the haunting question of why. I trust you will feel the hope and discover the encouragement I have found. I pray that you, too, shall find help. Healing for your broken spirit. Weary mind. Tired body.

I have shared the problems I faced. I have described the means that God used in my life to lead me out of pathos and pain. I have traced my path to peace, and explored the steps that strengthened and moved me to growth and freedom.

As I have shown my struggles, I have also testified to the power of God. Whatever pain I have experienced, I have found He was present. To comfort. Support. Strengthen. And, throughout my experiences, my awareness of His presence has deepened. The very real, vital and vibrant presence of the Christ has led me to triumph and joy.

I have attempted to weave my spiritual beliefs and psychological insights into a mosaic of help for any who will listen, while they are yet in the dark—searching for this side of dawn.

My story is a familiar one, yet it is unique because it is individual to me. In coming to a greater understanding of myself, I have become more sensitive to my own needs, and therein to the needs of others. In sharing my story, I hope to help those still tossed in the turmoil of travail, while seeking to bring forth a new life for themselves.

> Peace I leave with you, my
> peace I give unto you. . . . Let
> not your heart be troubled,
> neither let it be afraid. (John 14:27)

This is the legacy Christ left. It is available to every Christian. Whether he is able to appropriate it or not depends in large measure upon his ability to remove the emotional blocks that have immobilized him. Blocks that have short-circuited his path to peace and power, and to individual potential. God in Christ came to give us peace, to set us free, and to fill us with joy. In Him it all resides. It is for us to reach up for all that is available.

God bless you in the search.

Acknowledgments

In this book, I have traced the continuing direction of God in my life. I now gratefully acknowledge His leading in the steps I've taken in the writing and publication of my story.

I am indebted to my friend Ms. Lorraine Slowik for her confidence in this endeavor, and because she was instrumental in my undertaking this project.

I am grateful for the encouragement and suggestions of my friend Mr. William Schoenberg, for many years a representative of Harper and Row, Publishers, who advised me how to proceed in the process of writing for publication.

I am especially appreciative of the meaningful assistance of Mr. Lloyd Hildebrand of the editorial department.

I am grateful for the encouragement of my friends, and for the reading of the original manuscript by my minister, Dr. Robert Bruce Pierce.

I wish to thank the Wheaton College and Judson

College libraries for their gracious assistance, as well as the Moody Bible Institute and the Billy Graham Evangelistic Association for their helpfulness.

I appreciate the courtesy of the Park Ridge Library, and the public libraries of Chicago, Evanston, Morton Grove, and Elgin.

I am grateful to my friends to whom I have referred in these pages; for my significant relationships with them, out of which grew their contributions to this book.

I cherish the ministry of the many Bible teachers, preachers and writers through whom I have had the privilege of learning and growing over the years. Their influence and inspiration have contributed significantly to the theology I now hold, a theology I have shared with my readers in the following pages.

I acknowledge with gratitude the authors and publishers listed in the credits and their quotations.

I am deeply indebted to the King James Version of the Holy Bible, from which all Scripture references are taken, unless otherwise indicated.

It is with profound gratitude that I dedicate this book to the glory of my Lord and Savior, Jesus Christ.

Reach for Tomorrow

1

Dark Is Not Forever

"I'm scared of the dark, 'cause I can't see what's comin'." Little Junior, wide-eyed with fear, told it like it was. Mirroring my feelings, he said it as I felt it. Like him, I was scared. My world had suddenly become dark, and I was frightened.

Darkness hung heavy. Draped with the unknown, it was threatening. I couldn't see what was coming. What was "out there"? In the vast uncharted wilderness of my tomorrows? Terror clawed at my emotions as I considered my uncertain future. Numbed with shock, I slid into a new, black world of fear and shadows.

The shining hope and blissful joy of my courtship and most of my marriage had been replaced by a shivering cold. A compelling silence. An oppressive stillness. It was as if the music had ended. As though the band had stopped playing. My marriage lay crumbled in the shambles of bits and pieces. And broken dreams.

An awesome foreboding swept over me as though

I was being enveloped by a chilling arctic blast. With its inward thrust, it carried me into what seemed like a cold cave of fear and helplessness.

Drifting into a sense of isolation, I was filled with dread. Dread as ominous as the dark Kansas clouds I'd seen roll over the western sky, bringing storms across the prairie. A gathering tempest had swept over our relationship, gaining momentum. Thundering across our marriage, it shattered our dreams. Dreams that had begun years before. Dreams we had shared together.

Now the nightmare was mine alone. My feelings and memories, my thoughts and dreams clustered bunchlike as I hovered in despair. Crushed, I could see no hope. And without hope, what remained? Without hope one dies.

Once upon our dreams there had been joy and caring. Concern and planning. We had been building together. Building for our tomorrow. The shared satisfactions had created a union that presumably was indestructible. Our oneness seemed formidable for any foe. Our unity could weather any storm, we thought, and our solidarity was not questioned. By us, or by others. Others admired our apparent marital bliss. Our visible congeniality. Yet, this conjugal bond had been vulnerable. Woundable. Exposed to the erosion of discontent, despair descended with its pall of destruction. It crushed what once we had believed to be our "marriage made in heaven." Our broken dreams and vanished hopes lay silent in the settling dust, as rubble beneath a bulldozer.

I had neither sought nor wished to be in the quagmire that seemed to swallow me. The unfairness was choking. The inequity appalling. I flinched at the injustice. Following the divorce proceedings I had knelt at the church's altar, crying out over and over, "I didn't want it!" Agonizing in pain that felt brutal, I did not understand. Feeling abandoned and alone, I viewed my ended marriage.

Shortly afterwards I received a letter from my daughter in California. She wrote:

> I can know but in a small way what you feel—the bewilderment, the hurt, the doubts, the fears, the loneliness. And you think you'll die—but you don't (remember?) And you think the world is at an end. And for a while it will be.
>
> But God has said His burdens *will not* be more than we can bear. I've already told you I know you are strong, inside . . . you are as attractive on the inside as you are on the outside, and as you grow, you will discover a whole new wonderful life.

I know you don't want it, you like the old one, and it's scary. But the same love of life that's inside me will push you toward it. . . .

Perhaps I am saying it all wrong. I hope not. I am sitting here as one individual, reaching out, trying to let you know I know it hurts. And I wish there were some way I could make it not have to be so. . . .

My yearnings would not alter my crisis. My marriage was over. I was divorced. Nothing could change that reality. Longing for the past or regretting the present were emotions that would drain the energy I needed for constructive change.

With myopic vision I viewed the desolate ruin and despair that overwhelmed me. I could not "see what was comin'." The silence of my future seemed to seal me in its own tomb of terror. No ripple of hope, no stirring of help stilled the panic of the present. Trembling in the chilling inner darkness, shadows of fear danced on my shattered spirit. Numbed by anesthetizing pain that penetrated laserlike beyond my awareness, I nevertheless sought answers to the why and the how of the disintegration of my marriage. For days I was dazed by disillusionment. I pulled the covers over my head. I wanted to hide. I cried, and I wanted to die.

Fear and dread hung suspended in an air of incredulity at my inescapable sorrow. My irretrievable loss. My heavy heart pounded like angry waves dashing against huge boulders. My icy hands, with their sweaty palms, trembled. I had been plunged suddenly into this chaotic morass of separation and divorce. Terrified at facing life alone, it no longer held meaning for me. The desire to live had been snuffed out when my world fell apart. If I had to live alone, I did not want to live.

With the passage of time my feelings of loneliness were only to grow deeper. The silent watch of this night of torment in my life lasted as though forever. The clock of life ticked on. Graying dawn was yet far away.

The dark of midnight was long. Each night meshed into the next, linking discouragement, depression and despair. The very thought of dawn could not touch my troubled mind as I moved mechanically through this seemingly unending, vast wasteland of midnight. Any light at the end of the tunnel was a concept I could not then comprehend. I could not find the silver lining every cloud is supposed to have. I did not allow thoughts of hope to help. These were concepts that could not penetrate the fog of my fear. The "promise of tomorrow" seemed just words. Words that glided over the surface of my feelings. Feelings that were frozen in a frenzy of fear. Fear and loneliness. The loneliness of that far side of dawn.

My feeling of loneliness merely deepened in the company of others. Rather than assuaging my sense of emptiness, groups or crowds emphasized my solitariness. Happy couples in their togetherness enjoyed that same kind of sharing I once had known. Each was the important other, the significant someone. Someone who cared. Young couples were full of hope and dreams. Hope, the stuff of which dreams are made, crowded out distrust or fear. Like a ribbon of desert highway, the years stretched before them. Older generations were delighting in the fulfillment of their plans and goals. Memories were in the making while dreams were being realized. Devoted couples were celebrating anniversaries I would never reach with the man I thought would be by my side for life. These milestones, reflections in the pool of life, allow us to see the past, feel today and hope for tomorrow.

Christmas became the loneliest time of all. The first year as I searched for a small tree, I choked away the tears and fled from several stores. Memories of happy Christmases past were too poignant. The years that built those memories and solidified a bond that no judge could free. No document could undo. Loneliness, in torrents of despair sweeping across me, carried away any joy. It left my bereft spirit bathed in hopelessness. The little white tree I finally found shined in its adornment of twinkling golden lights and garlands. But their rays caught only glistening tears, reflecting the loss of love and the promise gone.

Driving to that first Christmas Eve celebration alone was dreary. I wept as the engine purred. The miles ticked on as my thoughts clamored for Christmas Eves of the past. That mystical moment of the year in its hushed splendor, silent wonder and warm mystique surely should succor souls everywhere! But the lights and songs of the season left only emptiness. A hollow hole, hewn from hope withdrawn. Only longing for love remained. Love given. And love received.

New Year's Eve brought the solitary midnight moment when for twenty-nine years we had kissed the New Year in as lovers do. I hungered for happiness. I craved contentment. I yearned for lasting love. I longed to be somebody special to somebody. I wished for the love of a good man who would value me above all others. I wanted and needed to give. I ached to receive.

How cozy my life had been! How snug it had seemed under the blanket of marriage, shielded from many harsh realities that beleaguer the woman alone. How secure I had felt on the inside of matrimony! Belonging. Enjoying a special place in the heart of a special person.

Now life was cold. Damp as a misty moor in the foggy twilight. Gray. Empty. I yearned for the significant partner in my life. I longed for the man with whom I had shared so many years and treasured dreams; in whose love I had delighted. Whose companionship I had enjoyed. Now, only the empty feeling of loneliness remained. The gnawing ache that accompanies loss.

I was resentful of man's frailty and his ability to hurt so deeply. Disillusioned, I vowed never again to trust so completely. In giving my whole self to our relationship, I could not understand a lesser return.

I was angry at society with its facade. I was bitter at those who, calling themselves Christians, had a thin concept of the love of which Jesus spoke. I was cynical at some church leaders who, as they sought to help heal the brokenhearted, avoided and neglected divorcees. I was hurt by alleged friends who declined to associate now with a divorcee. Fearing the stigma they attached to divorce would rub off on them, they drifted away.

I thank God for the friends who stayed close. My few genuine friends accepted me into their families. They gave themselves in love and emotional support.

They affirmed me. Even though I was a divorced person. They loved unconditionally as Jesus loved. Ten years later, we still share warm, close relationships. Without these friends my days would have been darker. My crisis more cruel.

Did I doubt God in my tragedy? Was I angry at Him? Did I deny Him? Or reject my faith? I did not love God less. But I did not understand. I was torn by many questions. I could not perceive why He had let me suddenly be alone. I did not understand why God had allowed it. Why had He permitted my marriage of so many years to end? Why had my attempt at happiness failed? Why? These were questions for which I had no answers. If I understood, I did not feel with my heart. If I perceived, I did not respond from my being.

I did not recognize when dawn finally began to break for me. Recovery crept up slowly, and spawned a strength overriding my weakness. It broke through almost imperceptibly. Unnoticed. It is not always possible to detect the first rays of dawn's light. But as morning breaks gradually upon earth's horizon, so also the process of healing began slowly. Very slowly. Little by little the hope and promise of a new life were beginning to dawn.

I first noticed it as my outlook began to change. Slowly, my world was enlarging. Enough to include new friends. I was less occupied with my own complicated world. My thoughts were focusing beyond myself. Weighty problems still needed solving. But the heavy load had lightened. The nightmares were fewer. As thunder fading into the distance, the bad dreams were moving on. No longer did I draw the covers over my head. There was less need to hide. I was coming out of my cave of incredulity. I was emerging from my cocoon of disbelief. Moving away from the weakness that had almost overwhelmed me, I was inching my way into more strength than weakness. Strength that was preparing me for a new tomorrow. Dawn was eventually beginning to break.

> The dawn should inspire shouts of anticipation—the coming of morning brings us a fresh page of life with nothing written on it. . . . It is ours to make of it what we will, to write well or ill. . . . Today is full of wonders to be appreciated . . . at the dawn of every morning there is a summons, "something is waiting, go and find it." . . . Command the morning with a mind alive with vital thoughts and inspiring images. Venture into each new day with a mind aware of something waiting to be found.[1]

---

[1] Dr. Harold Blake Walker, "Command the Morning," sermon preached at the First Presbyterian Church, Evanston, Illinois, and later appearing in *The Chicago Tribune*.

Now I was beginning not only the dawn of a new morning. The rest of my life was emerging out of the pain of the past. The dawn of my future was breaking. Light was looming. At last. Out of the hurt of the hours I'd wept away. Out of the dreams and hopes I had seen dashed on the rocks of life. I was learning it is possible to bring triumph out of tragedy, strength out of sorrow. I was experiencing that God has not promised to take away sorrow, but to turn it into joy.

> Your sorrow shall be turned into joy.
> (John 16:20)

The very thing that has caused the sorrow becomes the very source of the joy. Now this unwanted and feared divorce, which had caused my sorrow and pain, was to become the very source of a deeper level of joy. By divine metamorphosis the sorrow-turned-joy would reveal a new dimension. How this divorce with all its anguish could bring the faintest degree of joy had escaped me. Joy that had disappeared from my life.

But my sadness was being eclipsed by faint rays of hope. A thin glimmer of joy shined through the gray. Joy that broke through the diminishing darkness. Emerging out of this sorrow was the deep-seated joy He had promised. Gradually the process of healing was beginning to bring the promise. The promise of joy.

Emerson said:

> This time, like all times, is a very good one, if we but know what to do with it.[2]

I stood on the threshold of discovering how this time—this lonely, empty time—could be a good time. I was ready to learn what to do with it.

God defines it:

> Moreover we know that to those who love God, who are called according to His plan, everything that happens fits into a pattern for good. (Rom. 8:28, Phillips)[3]

I wavered on the edge of discovering that this time of anguish could "fit into a pattern for good." The good time God promised. I was ready to experience how this time could be good. Productive. Fulfilling. Satisfying.

One of the most courageous persons who ever

---

[2]Ralph Waldo Emerson, "The American Scholar", as quoted in *Great Treasury of Western Thought,* edited by Mortimer J. Adler and Charles Van Doren, R.R. Bowker Company, New York, New York. Copyright © 1977 by Xerox Corporation.

[3]J.B. Phillips, *The New Testament in Modern English*, Revised Edition. © J.B. Phillips 1958, 1960, 1972, MacMillan Publishing Co., Inc., New York, New York.

lived, Helen Keller, said:

> When one door of happiness closes, another opens; but often we look so long at the closed door that we do not see the one which has been opened for us.[4]

My door of happiness had closed, as I wandered in the bleak wilderness of separation and divorce. But a glimmer of light now streamed from the opening door of opportunity. It was for me to see what had been opened. To peer beyond. Dawn was beginning to break.

---

[4] Helen Keller, *We Bereaved* (New York: Leslie Fulenwider, Inc., 1929), p. 23.

2
On My Own

A journey to California was a gift from my mother. Offering me the plane ticket, she envisioned a helpful, healing visit to my daughter, living then near Fresno. The warm sun of the fertile San Joaquin Valley, and the serenity of the small, tidy town of Visalia, provided a retreat wherein I could absorb the hurt I felt and regain perspective on my life.

On relaxing jaunts we threaded our way through orange groves, lingered beside rushing mountain streams and climbed in the foothills of the Sierra Nevada Mountains. Reaching out in compassion, my daughter was reassuring. Her companionship and sharing supported me in warmth and understanding, in these days that dangled before me the possibility of a dawn yet to be.

However, my struggle was not yet over. My hurt was still raw. The shattered bits and pieces of my fragmented life had splintered around me like slivers of broken glass. My fractured emotions erupted in torrents of tears. I drifted in doleful dreams while distraught and disillusioned. My feelings had grown as fragile as finest crystal. I was living on the edge of crisis.

Returning from my vacation, I once again faced the frightening present. I focused on my priorities, and accepted the fact that work was a necessity. Though unsure of myself and bewildered, I began to interview for employment. Knowing what I did *not* want in a job, I was not sure of what I *did* want. Questioning how I could at this time cope with a career, I took the risk and accepted a position offered me. Receptionist and switchboard operator seemed an appropriate reentry opportunity. But how would I find the necessary composure, while this ache was still so commanding? The hurt was so excruciatingly real. I was afraid I would cry in public.

At one moment, recoiling in fear, but with tottering strength, I began my new job. An officer of the company remarked to me later that when I was hired he had observed, "She will only last a week, she's so afraid." Remaining on that job for ten years before moving on, I proved that work was therapeutic. I demonstrated that I could rise above the malaise that was strangling me, beyond the defeat that sought to immobilize.

Also, part of the frightening present was living

ON MY OWN

alone. For living alone became lonely at times. So lonely it was scary. Living with no commitment to another meant most major and minor crises were managed solely by me. Those intense pressures that made me push the panic button: crises concerning my children, my aging parent, potential financial catastrophe, personal illness. In these major moments, loneliness was frightening.

In the minor trivia of life, loneliness gave way to forlornness. It was TV as a dinner partner. Watching the ball game alone. Viewing the sunset by myself. Thinking I heard a burglar at three o'clock in the morning. Trying to unstick a stuck zipper. Attempting to scratch my own back. Not getting an opinion on a new outfit. All projected the solitariness of life!

Loneliness was arriving home to the deafening silence of emptiness. Overwhelming stillness. However, for the first ten years after my divorce, I knew the welcome greeting of my beautiful Persian cat. As I turned the key in the lock, I encountered the softly changing moment when my faithful feline friend would soothe away my loneliness with his royal reception. Shaded silver with intense emerald green eyes, he lived to be twenty-one years of age before being put to sleep. Not a record. But beyond the ordinary. A geriatric accomplishment for a cat. I believe the God who notes the sparrow's fall extended the life of my pet, through his many physical crises, to brighten my life alone.

Yes, I have known loneliness. Believing I could learn to deal with it, I faced it. I allowed myself to feel it. I accepted the fact that I *was* feeling lonely. Very lonely. I found that, in time, the intensity of the feeling passed. I discovered that allowing myself to feel the loneliness, to acknowledge its existence, and to ride out the empty, desolate feeling, as riding the waves of the sea, were necessary steps in the process of becoming.

I sensed the strength I felt in the midst of that loneliness was greater than mine alone. I realized a power beyond my own, inching me toward new growth. I repeated the Scripture:

> When he putteth forth His own sheep, he goeth before them. (John 10:4)

> We are his people, and the sheep of his pasture. (Ps. 100:3)

I recalled a painting that hung on the wall in the dining room of my childhood home. The shepherd in the pastoral setting was making his way over the rolling hills and through a valley. He was leading his flock of sheep as they huddled in a group together behind him; the shepherd, staff in hand, strolled in front. The sheep followed. The painting portrayed peace and safety.

Now, I was realizing the same sense of security in knowing that Christ, the Shepherd, had gone ahead. He was leading me. Up front. I could depend on help over the rough spots. He had gone before. I could count on the dark places becoming lighter. The steep places becoming gentle. In safety I could move forward. Each situation I would encounter was one through which He had already gone. This sense of security deepened my trust. Calmed my fears. Quieted my anxieties. My days were becoming better. And they were destined to improve.

As the freshness of spring was chasing the winter of 1969 into the past, on a particular Sunday morning, sparkling in its newness, I turned my radio dial and discovered the morning broadcast of the Chicago Temple. This was my introduction to Dr. Robert Bruce Pierce, the pastor.

I had not been attending public worship during the early weeks of my separation. Though needing the help of the church, in my devastation I had lacked the courage to worship in public. In the past, church had been an integral part of my life. For the fifteen years my husband had been in the active pastorate, I had been in a special relationship with the church. As first lady of the manse, my primary interest had been in the church and its outreach. The parishioners and the programs. The missionaries and the ministry.

Now it was difficult for me to separate the beliefs I cherished from the disillusionment I was experiencing. My sorrow was too recent for me to be objective. In despair from my loss, the ability to be detached was clouded. It was difficult to differentiate between the support of the ministry and the hurt I had experienced.

As I found strength to return to church, I discovered a refuge in the Chicago Temple, the First United Methodist Church. I saw in Dr. Pierce a brilliant man with compassion and sensitivity. I found in him a minister who accepted me as a person. A divorced person. Nonjudgmental, he was supportive. In his message and ministry I found comfort and strength. I received help. Dynamic and didactic, he effected impact and influence. I respected and admired him.

One of the first sermons I heard him preach expressed the thought:

> The most creative thing in us is our capacity to believe a thing in. Faith and belief can actually bring a thing to pass. Believing will make it so. It is different

than wishing or hoping. It makes you a doer.[1]

Here was another facet of faith! To believe I was a partner with God in making a thing happen! I was definitely aware of what I desired. I yearned for a depth of relationship. For the warm glow genuine friendship provides. For the sense of belonging. For abiding love. Tender concern.

And I was a partner with God! My faith could bring a thing to pass! Not just wishing. Or dreaming. Or thinking. But doing. Involvement. Being involved would cause me to become a doer. Learning to believe a thing in was to let hoping give way to productive doing. Action. Movement.

But relating to others is where it would begin. Beyond the surface feelings. Association. In depth. That I might know others, and that others might know me for whom I really am! In an intensity beyond the superficial. The shallow.

But I discovered anew how slowly each moves. I was finding again that building a meaningful relationship is a very gradual process. I was realizing once more that solid friendships are formed through learning to trust.

And to trust another means risk. It meant risking

---

[1] "Believing a Thing In!", preached May 25, 1969, in the Chicago Temple, The First United Methodist Church, Dr. Robert Bruce Pierce, Pastor.

again my feelings. If I wanted the joy of loving, I must risk the possible hurt. Trouble. Fear.

Somewhere along the way I remembered what Jesus said:

> Let not your heart be troubled. . . . be not afraid. (John 14:1; Matt. 14:27)

Let not! It was up to me. It was within my power to be troubled. Agitated. Hurt. Fearful. Or not to be. It was within my own control. Worry was not brought about by forces outside of myself. It was my own determination whether I would worry or not. I *could* control what happened inside me. I *could* choose how to react. I *was* able not to be afraid. External pressures did *not* produce my reaction. It was up to *me* whether or not I *let* it happen. If I ordered my thoughts, and then committed them to God, calm followed. Tension left. It *was* possible to relax in God. He was saying I have the power to choose whether I will be troubled, afraid and hurt, or calm, peaceful and secure. I was learning to believe a thing in. To become a doer. I was learning to again risk possible hurt in getting close enough to love.

And, meanwhile, I also was discovering an increased awareness of myself. Of what I *felt*. I was taking time to enjoy the roses. To watch a sunset.

Relish the fresh air. Talk to a child. Listen to the sounds of music. Pay attention to the little things. As I grew in feeling, there began to come gradual healing. And, inevitably growth. Growth that revealed itself in various ways.

As I settled back in my chair, or curled beside the fire at the end of the day, I was beginning to sense a new appreciation for others. I was realizing my new-found friends were sharing themselves. Their joys and achievements. Their problems. Our lives touched, if only briefly. They gave a bit of themselves. I was aware of my increased interest in them. More understanding. Of others. Of myself. I came to appreciate how much we have to give to each other. I discovered my new friends were genuinely concerned. Caring. They helped me to feel less lonely and less afraid.

I was also discovering the difference between loneliness and aloneness. Loneliness was the empty, gnawing sensation of loss. The aching awareness of being completely by myself. Feeling desolate. Isolated. Loss, however fleeting or sustained, brings a feeling of emptiness. A void. Loneliness.

Aloneness can be distinctly different. It embraces a solitariness. This can be threatening in generating a feeling of helplessness. Forlornness. But to one whose self-image is healthy, adequate and equal to the strain of life, aloneness has a healthful, positive meaning. It implies separateness. Apartness. Aloneness says, "I am aware of me and my apartness, and it doesn't frighten me. I do not feel threatened by it. I can handle solitude. I can even enjoy it. I like me well enough to spend time with me!"

But solitude *is* threatening to many. *Chicago Tribune* columnist Bob Greene writes:

> A check with psychologists who deal in studying the family showed that there is an increasing interest in the phenomenon in the psychological community.
>
> "It's really interesting that you should ask me about that," said Dr. Jean Goldsmith of the Center for Family Studies. "I have just finished a study of divorced adults . . . who are living with their parents now, rather than living alone."
>
> It is not just divorced people who are moving back with their parents. . . . Dr. Kathleen Sheridan, associate professor of clinical psychiatry at Northwestern University [said,] "People . . . return to a place of safety—their parents. . . . Going back . . . represents, to them a healing process. . . . home is the only safe haven

they know. They're saying, "I'm so wounded, I need to heal . . . and I'm going back to the only place where I know I will be safe."[2]

The hurt needs to heal. And some may need to return home. But I believe the answer seldom lies entirely in going home. For myself, I am grateful that in the healing process, I did not seek shelter in returning home.

Mildred Newman and Bernard Berkowitz write:

> An adult . . . often needs aloneness to grow, to get to know himself and develop his powers. Someone who cannot tolerate aloneness is someone who doesn't know he's grown up. . . . What fresh air we breathe when we take possession of our own separateness, our own integrity! That's when adult life really begins.[3]

There was still another facet to this frightening present. My most recurring frustration was the thwarting of my own thrust toward life. Friends, in seeking to protect and shield, were often

---
[2] Bob Green, *The Chicago Tribune,* January 3, 1979, Section 4, p. 2.
[3] Mildred Newman, Bernard Berkowitz, *How To Be Your Own Best Friend* (New York: Random House, Inc., © 1971), pp. 30, 31.

destructive by their discouragement. You're going to get hurt was a frequent warning. I was perceived as vulnerable. Fragile. From the naiveté of my sheltered past.

Smothered in my urge toward life, I felt stifled in my attempts at self-fulfillment. Temporarily, inner growth was curtailed as I focused on defending myself. My position, my plans and goals. I valued the concern of friends. Their love. But I longed for the kind of love that would allow me to be free. Love me enough to let me be me! Don't smother the fire of faith I have in myself. Differ, but don't discourage. Love me enough to let me discover life for myself. Have faith in me. Belief in me is the greatest gift you can give to me. Don't corner me into a need to defend my decisions! Don't compound my struggle to be strong. Love me enough to accept me as I am!

Eventually, however, I outgrew the need to defend my decisions. I moved toward loving my friends enough to accept them as they were. With *their* needs. Even the need to protect me. I was growing within. And in my relationships. Learning better how to live. I learned just to *be*. To be me. Not what anyone thought I should be. Or do. I was discovering how to succeed at living alone. I was taking possession of my own separateness.

I recall an experience at the close of my earlier

California trip. It had proven to be one of those seemingly insignificant times that nevertheless remains beneath the surface. Nesting in the unconscious. Ready to jump out later.

Pausing in the ladies lounge in the Fresno airport, I had glanced in the full-length mirror. I remembered then a thought of Dr. Maxwell Maltz:

> Look at yourself in the mirror. . . . See the person behind the face. . . . Keep this image of yourself alive—be good to yourself and look into your treasure box of experiences for your successes, for your good moments, for your winning feelings. . . . As you look into your mirror tell yourself that you will go forward . . . strengthening yourself, supporting yourself. It is this sense of self that will help you to live creatively. . . . You will be building the self-image which you need for resourceful living.[4]

Now I was finding within me resources to cope. A courage beneath the level of my conscious understanding.

But the times when I felt successful were

---

[4] Maxwell Maltz, M.D., F.I.C.S., *Creative Living for Today* (New York: Trident Press, 1967) pp. 16-18.

transitory at first. Courage ebbed and flowed. The panicky feeling feverishly returned as the tide of courage went out. I had glimpsed the dawn, but a graying mist had crept in. The lengthening shadows had caused me to forget the wonderful warmth of the sun. My brief, sweet moment in daylight.

Slowly I began to push my self-defeat button less. Successes surprised me more often. Courage grew as I alone was in control of myself and my new life style. I was responsible for me. I was making my own decisions.

At first I was terrified. The bigger the decision, the greater the nauseous fear. Little by little, however, confidence crept in with each experience. Eventually I discovered it was exciting to be managing me! The feeling was fascinating. Like riding a bicycle for the first time. Or swimming alone in deep water. Or receiving the keys to the car. Driving off alone. Freedom, A buoyancy that carried me above my fear. Being in charge of myself had its own reward. I was glimpsing capacities of which I had not been aware. Dr. Harold Blake Walker writes:

> Nobody is inferior to any other in the economy of God, and the clue to triumphant living is in making the most of

whatever capacities we possess. We can be content to be less than ourselves and waste our possibilities, or we can choose to be more than ourselves, doing what we must to achieve what we ought.[5]

I was seeking to make the most of my own capabilities. I was doing it all *my* way. Sometimes, however, my way was unwise. Because it was not God's way. I made inappropriate decisions. I chose the wrong friends. I was impatient. I ran when I should have walked. I walked when I should have stood still. These were the times I stumbled along on my own. Disregarding God.

Nevertheless, in my neglect I discovered anew His patience. He allowed me to find myself, discover His will, and follow my commitment to Him. He allowed me to learn. He permitted me the right to be wrong. I discovered the discipline that leads to freedom.

I began to pursue new interests. First, I pondered the things that needed sorting out. What self-defeating habits had I hugged to myself? What during marriage had I embraced in the name of duty? For the sake of companionship? I realized I was shuttling back and forth within a rut. Mired in

---

[5]Dr. Harold Blake Walker, "Feeling Inferior," *Chicago Tribune Magazine*, August 27, 1978.

routine. Habit. And not even my own choices. Discontentment with the old way swept over me. I desired to break out. Discover what it was I *really* liked. Exchange my likings for my "have tos." Find what really pleased *me*. Explore what I wanted for my own enjoyment and enrichment.

Fresh motivations teased. Desires and dreams drew me to the delightful edge of adventure. New outlets of creative expression excited me. Evening school classes challenged. I returned to writing.

Recording my feelings had long been a way of expressing myself. It was reassuring. Reaffirming. Writing helped me sort out my feelings. Clarify my thinking as decisions were needed. Release intense emotion. Focus my thoughts and feelings, allowing me freedom to use reason. Maneuver things into perspective.

Meanwhile, in this frightening present, I also came to terms with rejection. At the time of my divorce I had not isolated that emotion. Nor realized its strength. Aware then of the hurt, and conscious of the anger, only now could I face the fact of rejection.

The sense of repudiation as a wife was painful anguish. I cringed at being denied the privilege of being a wife. I felt cut off. The abrupt ending of bringing love and tenderness hurt. The resulting isolation was tormenting. Passion turned to dread.

Rejection careened in destructive force, eroding my self-esteem. Leaving me feeling unwanted. Unloved. And unlovable.

Nevertheless, I came to appreciate that although I had lost my marriage, I still had myself. Dr. Frank Kimper writes:

> You are precious simply because you are. You were born that way. To see that, and to be grasped by the reality of it, is to love. . . . Claiming love for yourself is the real secret. . . . You are you. Claim yourself. Be who you are. You are a person of worth. Own yourself. Recognize what you are. . . . Be who you are before God and man.[6]

I am precious because I have been made in the image of God. Redeemed by Christ. I am precious because God loves me. I am of value. Worthwhile. God paid a tremendous price for me, therefore, I am of value to Him. To myself. To others. Because God provided the basis for it, I have valid reason to believe I am worthwhile. Though rejected, I am still of value. Because God loved me and placed value on me, I can love myself.

---

[6] David Augsburger, *Caring Enough to Confront: The Love-Fight* (Scottdale, Pa.: Herald Press, 1973), pp. 46, 109, 111.

Love of self differs from selfishness, which disregards others. The Bible says:

> Thou shalt love thy neighbor as thyself.
> (Lev. 19:18)

As you love yourself. The love of self of which God spoke is unalterably linked with the love of neighbor. Love others as I love myself. Be myself. Develop myself.

Dale Carnegie writes:

> Be yourself. . . . When [Irving] Berlin and [George] Gershwin first met, Berlin was famous but Gershwin was a struggling composer. . . . Berlin . . . offered Gershwin a job. . . . "But don't take the job," Berlin advised. "If you do, you may develop into a second-rate Berlin. But if you insist on being yourself, some day you'll become a first-rate Gershwin."[7]

My sensitivity following rejection was beginning to fade. My sense of self-esteem was returning. Acknowledging my own identity, I was learning to be me. Recognizing myself for the person I was brought an exhilarating glow of self-acceptance.

---

[7] Dale Carnegie, *How to Stop Worrying and Start Living* (New York: Simon & Schuster, Inc., 1948), p. 125.

Loretta Young, favorite actress of many for years on television's "The Loretta Young Show," writes of an interview she had before she became a star, with the head of the studio, Mr. Al Rockett, who said,

> You *are* going to be a star. Someday.... It won't be easy. We'll help. But most of all—and always—you'll have to be yourself, believe in yourself. Remember that, Gretchen, when it's real tough and real lonely. Be yourself. Believe in yourself. Make yourself responsible....[8]

The more self-awareness I experienced, the greater the need for its expression. An inevitable outgrowth of that need was the creation of something uniquely mine.

One day, paying attention to the longings nudging me, I settled back on the sofa. A dear friend listened as I announced, "I could write a book! I'm *going* to write a book! Something that will say, 'This is me! *My* story! If God has given me these years to live, and I haven't learned anything, it doesn't say very much about me, does it?"

---

[8] Loretta Young, as told to Helen Ferguson. *The Things I Had to Learn* (New York: Bobbs-Merrill Co., Inc., a Subsidiary of Howard W. Sams & Co., Inc., 1961) p. 72.

Sharing my enthusiasm, she saw the birth of my thought. Soon after, I began the writing of this book. I knew it would be a declaration of my faith in God, traced through the significant moments of my life. I believed I had something to say to the glory of God. I discovered it also was therapeutic as I recalled the positive that produced growth, and the strength that grew out of the sorrow.

Somerset Maugham said, after writing *Of Human Bondage*:

> The book did for me what I wanted, and when it was issued to the world . . . I found myself free forever from those pains and unhappy recollections. I put into it everything I then knew and having at last finished it prepared to make a fresh start.[9]

As the famous author found freedom in writing of his past, I too found, in writing, release from the pain and loss experienced during my separation and divorce.

To record my feelings was a contribution to the world of which I am a part. My feelings are unique to me. No one else has feelings exactly like mine. No one comes from the same background. No one

---
[9] Somerset Maugham, *The Summing Up* (New York: Doubleday, Doran and Co., Inc., 1938), pp. 191-92.

has experienced an identical set of circumstances. No one can feel precisely the same as I. Sharing these feelings is my gift to others. A legacy.

To relate my selfness was reaffirming to me. I wrote not as the wife of anyone. I wrote as a single woman. I recorded what it was like to be plunged to the depths of despair after twenty-nine years of marriage to one man. I related how it felt to rise again, phoenixlike. To emerge a new and stronger person. To be able to say, "I was there. But, by the grace of God, here I am today."

Dr. Paul Tournier wrote:

> No one discovers himself in solitude, by turning inward on himself and by analyzing himself. It is by giving one's self that one finds himself.[10]

This record of my feelings, sharing of that which hurt along with that which helped—this giving of myself—was for me an integral part of the process of becoming.

It was reaffirming for me to say, "I am conquering the crisis. I am proud of me and what I am doing. I've come a long, long way. That is how it was. This is how it is. It is, was and will always be,

---

[10]Paul Tournier, *Secrets*, trans. Joe Embry (Richmond: John Knox Press, © 1965 by M.E. Bratcher).

too soon to quit. It is possible to live again—to live happily again."

Realizing and building upon this core strength, it continued to emerge again and again. I was growing. Changing. Being on my own. Living alone. Surviving. Discovering my resources.

Gail Sheehy writes:

> . . . learning to live alone is not just transitionally good; it can also be essentially good . . . one has no idea if the resources are there to survive as an individual, it can be a self-affirming experience to discover that the answer is yes . . . if we don't change, we don't grow. If we don't grow, we are not really living. Growth demands a temporary surrender of security. . . . The courage to take new steps allows us to let go of each stage with its satisfactions and to find the fresh responses that will release the richness of the next. The power to animate all of life's seasons is a power that resides within us.[11]

---

[11]Reprinted by permission of E.P. Dutton from *Passages: Predictable Crises in Adult Life* by Gail Sheehy. Copyright © 1974, 1976 by Gail Sheehy. Excerpted from pp. 349, 359, 353, and 354.

3
Another Dimension

Learning long ago that God is too wise and too loving to err in anything He does or permits, I did not doubt Him in all of the crises of my separation and divorce. I had already experienced in earlier years the direct leading of God in my life. In past days He had proven His promises. My former experiences of sensitivity to His will were not presently forgotten. Awareness of His direction before was supporting me now as I continued to struggle alone.

I vividly recall the direction given my husband and me before his graduation from college. Then, as we were nestled in our tiny honeymoon apartment in a quiet midwestern town, we had contemplated our next move. Cozily comfortable in our newly married life, and quiet in the warmth of our love, we had reflected on seminary days ahead. Tiptoeing among the advantages and disadvantages, we finally had opted for an eastern school with its exceptional opportunities. The meshing of their overtures with our needs had convinced us that God had a plan for us beyond the Appalachians! On the banks of the Schuylkill. Though others tried to dissuade us during those days, we had remained firm in our conviction that it was God's direction. Our belief then was continuously confirmed in time.

God's guidance then instilled confidence in me. A certainty that He knew my need and had made provision to meet it. My trust in His direction crystallized into a valuable dimension of my Christian faith. It stabilizes me even now if I question the present. When I become concerned for the future.

As I think back, the move to Pennsylvania significantly altered our lives. No other single decision was to affect our future to the degree of that commitment. Even today, decades later, I am conscious of the ongoing influence of that move. As I realize my values and make my own decisions now.

In the early forties Philadelphia was a city of heightened activity, during the time when my husband studied for the ministry there. Sudden blackouts and practice air raids then punctuated the nights. Music blared from USO centers, as army convoys rumbled over cobblestone streets. Those were the days of Coventry and Dunkirk,

Pearl Harbor and Rheims. Days that sobered the world, and nights that brought America to her knees. It was a period of change in the world. Change in our lives.

Now in my life alone, the changes I have faced have reminded me of the changes we experienced then. Discovering God's will and proceeding in faith at that time instilled faith that time only reinforced.

Back then in the forties, our destiny evidently lay in a change of denominational affiliation. Study of the Bible, together with the forceful ministry of the late Dr. Donald Grey Barnhouse, had opened for us exciting new vistas of biblical truth. We realized we were altering our doctrinal beliefs. We sensed our new convictions required the big step of a change in our theological position. It became essential that in preparing for leadership and instruction we study in a milieu of our enlarged perspective. Our affiliation needed to be transferred to the Presbyterian denomination.

I am convinced that, in those early years, if we had remained in the Midwest, we would not have altered our denominational commitment. Only in Philadelphia, with our exposure to Reformed theology occurring so persuasively, could we have effected that major change. Change that shaped all our tomorrows. Sensitivity to the will of God at that time moved us to a basic change of commitment, as it had also brought us to that particular place. Philadelphia, the birthplace of our nation, was also the place where our first child, a girl, was born.

In retrospect I realize that during the period of my separation and the early days of my divorce, I leaned heavily on the faith I had found in these earlier years. I remembered the evidences of His love. The direction He gave us in those early years together.

I recall the significant decision when we changed our theological position. My husband transferred his studies to Princeton Theological Seminary. Midway between Philadelphia and New York, the quaint little town of Princeton, New Jersey, charmed us as we called it home for several years. Never did we doubt our earlier decision to go to Philadelphia, nor our decision to move on to Princeton. A significant, soft flow of peace settled over us then with assurance that we were in God's designated place. That peace never left us.

It was this same sense of direction I now needed in my continuous struggle alone. Significant signs carpeting a path to peace. I was trusting God for a sense of sureness. A certainty that would remain stable. Even as the decisions of those early years had continued constant.

I have not forgotten the indecision that faced us back in the forties as my husband graduated from seminary. With no commitment to a pastorate, we headed back to the Midwest for a short visit with my parents. Not knowing where we would eventually settle, we finally set out, pointing our car north.

Weaving a web of circumstance then, God made His plan unmistakably clear. A phone call intercepted us en route. An interview followed. A congregation acted. The First Presbyterian Church of a small northern town became our first pastorate.

I can still see the oversized house, designated the minister's home, that greeted us. A rambling assortment of rooms. Foreboding to a young family of only three. We requested permission to rent a small place suitable for our few needs. Rentals were very scarce, we were told, and probably impossible to find. But within one-half hour of "house hunting," as an arrow to its mark, we zeroed in on a smaller, charming place that became our first home. Again we marveled at God going before us. Four years of our lives were devoted to this pastorate—our first charge—and it was here that our son was born. Indeed, my past is peppered with the promises of God, fulfilled as I followed His leading.

An incident recorded in the Gospel of Luke

illustrates the guidance of God. Nudging us toward Him, it reveals the way in which He directs. God sent Peter and John to prepare the Passover. When they asked Jesus where to prepare it, He told them to enter the city, and

> there shall a man meet you, bearing a pitcher of water; follow him. . . . And they went, and found as he had said unto them. (Luke 22:10, 13)

Often in my life God has given me an unmistakable sign. A "man with a pitcher." He has sent a friend. A stranger. A letter. A phone call. Perhaps just an unexplained happening. Like the day I was able to "go back home."

The belief is that one *cannot* go back home. That it is not possible to recapture the past. That one is unable to relive his former experiences. The accompanying emotions cannot be felt again. Perhaps. Yet, there are joys to be captured and lessons to be learned from returning to one's childhood home. Going home can be appreciated. An emotional involvement with the mystique of the past has its own reward.

It was a lazy Sunday afternoon as I walked by the home of my childhood years. The pull of the past was strong. Sufficient for me to hesitate and peer at the empty house. Obviously, no one now lived there. The former owners, through gross neglect, had allowed the grand old place to deteriorate. The peeling paint hung stalactitelike in sheets pointing toward the ground. The rusted gutters were a sea of gaping holes, and the frame sections were dilapidated in their decay. Sadly, I gazed on the current disarray of the house that captivated me with such incredible enchantment.

I strode up the walk and climbed the creaking frame steps. Looking inside, tender recollections darted from the corners of my mind. I listened to the murmur of the memories. Haunting moments leaped out of the past. I was home. Pausing in reflection, memories washed over me. My feet were frozen in time.

A car drove up with a couple inside. Beckoning, the man queried, "May I help you?" My thoughts spun around, bringing me back to the present. This man informed me he was the new owner. Again God lightened my life with a "man with a pitcher." If I had come back home one month sooner, he would not have been there. A month later, the structural changes he planned would have destroyed the inherent interest that captivated me! He could have been hostile to this trespasser. Or indifferent to my reason for being there. Hastily explaining my interest in the property, this landscape of my childhood, he and his wife graciously invited me inside to look around!

Never had I dreamed I could one day go back home—to the house of my childhood years. The familiar telltale signs remained. The walls and windows of my wonderful world, while somewhat worn, were welcome sights. Every corner held treasures of thought that threaded their way back through time to the toys, the trains and the teddy bears. I climbed the stairs to my bedroom. Then, with memories crowding out the present, I made my way up creaking steps that curled around corners to the musty attic. Beautiful in its cobwebby splendor, it reflected joys of childhood capers. The now empty, yet hallowed haven was dusty with the dreams of yesterday. A cavernous room, it captured the charm that had not been chased away by change. Sloping rafters, as silent sentinels, looked down upon a sacred season of life now past.

Leaving the house, I sauntered through the orchard. My feelings were confused. I was gripped with a sense of loss. I was stung by the pain of the poignancy of the past. That which had receded into history. Not unlike my feelings as a child when I thrilled to the ride on the observation platform of the Pullman car.

The wheels of the speeding train would hum as they roared over the rails. Beyond the last car, as the distance lengthened, the tracks seemed to merge—as if becoming one. Then, gradually disappearing, seemed to fade away. Lost on the horizon.

So now the past, as a mirage, had slipped away. Gone. Into the twilight of time. Forever.

Yet, not totally. The past never *really* leaves. It just seems to go. As the rails had not actually disappeared. Only apparently. They still existed, firmly fixed on the roadbed. So also, the past remains. It becomes incorporated into the present. I realized I had woven the good memories of my past with the actualities of the here and now. The strengths I had absorbed from former days had fused with the realities of the present. Dr. W. Hugh Missildine writes:

> What happened to the child you once were? Did he or she die? Was he outgrown and cast aside, along with old toys, overshoes and sleds? Was he somehow abandoned? Was he lost somewhere in Time, eventually forgotten? . . .
>
> The child you once were continues to survive inside your adult shell. . . . We are simultaneously the child we once were . . . and an adult who tries to forget the past and live wholly in the present. . . . Each of us carries within him his "inner

child of the past"—a set of feelings and attitudes brought from childhood. . . . "The child of the past" actually continues . . . to the very end of our lives.[1]

"Going home" enriched my life. That buoyant Sunday afternoon, as I met God's "man with a pitcher," a new perspective was provided as I dusted off the past. Savored the present. Hoped for tomorrow.

By His interventions God has made me aware of His planned purpose. I have seen beyond the person, the object or the situation, and recognized His messenger. Mysteries have melted. Convictions have constrained me as His message appeared. At times veiled, it always became clear. In my tomorrows I know I will see again in another time, another place, His "man with a pitcher." He has already sent ahead! In joy and laughter, through fear and pain, in loneliness and at times of decision or commitment, He inevitably sends to His own. He guided Israel with the cloud by day and the pillar of fire by night. Always He provides.

I am conscious of this direction in the minor as well as the major areas of my life. A glimpse of a bit of trivia illustrates my belief that God is also

---

[1] W. Hugh Missildine, M.D., *Your Inner Child of the Past* (New York: Simon & Schuster, 1963), pp. 13, 14, 20.

interested in the inconsequential events of our lives.

Intending to travel one evening to a small town where I had never been before, I did not relish driving the crowded expressways and maneuvering the various entrances and exists. Nor did I enjoy probing the dark for an exact address. While at my job during the day, a customer stood at my desk asking for a particular person in the company. Had the individual requested been available at that precise moment, I would not have had the opportunity for further conversation. But, because the customer was detained, he initiated conversation. Happening to mention where he lived, the town was the same to which I was driving in a few hours! Sharing with him my intended trip, he gave me specific directions and drew a small map. Reflecting on the facts, I realized that on the same day I intended for the first time to travel to a particular city, I encountered the only person in nine years that just "happened" to be from that city, who was detained at my desk, inclined to conversation, and able to give me detailed directions! Coincidence? Chance?

I believe such a minor incident illustrates the significance of detail. Nothing is inconsequential in the economy of God. I believe the God of the universe is a God of order and design for our individual lives. I believe things don't just happen. They're planned. I am convinced that God orders the pauses as well as the productivity in the life of every Christian.

> In all thy ways acknowledge him, and he shall direct thy paths. (Prov. 3:6)

> I will instruct thee and teach thee in the way which thou shalt go: I will guide thee with mine eye. (Ps. 32:8)

Not only does God guide the Christian, but He provides His presence. He is a constant reality. An immediate comfort. A reassuring help. This realization was calming.

A favorite song often soothed me with its soft reassurance. Like moonlight on a meadow, the melody lingered as the message imbedded itself in my mind and heart.

> I looked for Him
> In the soft summer rain,
> And He was there!

> When my world was dark
> And it all seemed in vain
> Yet He was there!

ANOTHER DIMENSION

> Then I saw Him
> In the desert sun
> And on the avenue—
>
> I could hear Him
> At the little church
> When two sweethearts
> Said, "I do."
>
> I looked for Him
> In the heart of a friend
> And He was there.
>
> It's so simple,
> Yet so wonderful
> Everybody—everywhere,
>
> Just look for Him
> And He'll be there![2]

I rediscovered this truth. If I lost the sense of God's presence, it was because I had moved aside. Not He. Wherever I was, if I looked for Him, He was there. When ill in a taxi as it crept along on the bulging expressway—locked between cars that

---

[2] "He Was There," Words and music by Jimmie Dodd, ASCAP. Copyright 1951, 1952; Copyright renewal 1979, 1980, Ruth Dodd Braun, Jaynar Music Publishing, 9636 Shoshone Avenue, Northridge, CA 91325. Used by permission.

hugged bumper to bumper—in a hospital corridor uneasily waiting in line to enter the surgery room, threatening with its stillness, searing lights and antiseptic smells; during the lonely night watch pierced by only the hourly chimes of the steeple clock, or in the waking moments of the dawn—I hummed the music and whispered the lyrics!

Just look for Him, and He'll be there!

He *is* there! I was learning a new dimension in practicing the presence of Christ.

4
Working It Out

There are times when it is appropriate to look back. Reflect. Assimilate the past, and learn from it. One of those times was now. Tracing back to the beginning of my faith in God. It all began in my youth. Though I had been impish as a child, and spirited as a young girl, I nevertheless had seriously considered the claims of God. Then trusting in Jesus Christ, I accepted His blood atonement as the only means of salvation from sin. I became a Christian.

> But God commendeth his love toward us, in that, while we were yet sinners, Christ died for us. (Rom. 5:8)

Experiences that illustrate God's direction in my life began almost immediately. I thirsted for knowledge of the Bible. Reading it inspired me. As it sharpened my spiritual senses, my faith in God deepened.

Soaring from the crest of a personal relationship with Jesus Christ, during high school days I encountered my first intense experience in trusting God. While a senior, I underwent a routine appendix operation. But, quite uncommonly, I developed acute peritonitis. This is an inflammation of the membrane that lines the abdominal cavity. Often this type of infection spreads, becoming fatal.

Concern grew as my hospital days lengthened. My fever climbed. As my condition worsened, it became critical. The pain and suffering were intense. My anxious family and friends, minister and congregation prayed. Miraculously, I believe, the infection localized, and the condition was dealt with surgically. Painful but necessary procedures were completed, and eventual healing began. Complete recovery followed.

It was during the weeks of recuperation that I realized my new appreciation for life. I had experienced the first basic lesson in trusting God for one of the ultimates: my life. Spanning the years, rainbowlike, the memory of the simplicity of my faith was a constant reminder that God brings glory from a cloud. The vitality of my faith then when a young girl has continued to throb with vibrancy as I remember God's power. His healing power. I realize He does not go off somewhere in the universe leaving me to myself. To discover my own way through the galaxy of my starry dreams and foolish fantasies.

The profound impact then now cushions the inevitable blows that are part of life. In my impressionable youth, the crisis had brushed by, leaving indelible imprints of faith. Faith that settled and became secure, laying a foundation for future shocks.

Later, during fifteen years in the active pastorate beside my husband, again many experiences propelled me to a maturing trust in God. He solved the myriad crises that relentlessly moved along within our parish. As pastor and wife we hovered between our own personal crises of daily living.

Each move to a new pastorate was initiated by a desire to determine the will of God. Resolving to discover His best for us, we prayed He would block that which was not His directive, perfect will. Conversely, that He would put before us that open door of which He spoke. Incredible were the signs He chose. Persons and places, as red flags, signaled His intervention.

During the lean years of meager income, our faith grew as limited resources dwindled. I learned to value pennies and to count them carefully to stretch my food budget. Though demeaned by some, pennies still seem to me more gold than copper. For the poor preacher, pennies often provided the difference between a meal or none at all.

Faith expanded in our years of ministry, and faith also bridged the span from marriage to divorce.

Recently I was asked what were the happiest and saddest moments of my life. My answers came swiftly. Undoubtedly, my sheerest happiness was the magical moment of my marriage. Seared in my memory is that hot summer evening when, standing in the church at the altar before the minister, I heard the cherished whisper, "I do love you, sweetheart!" The enchantment of the moment lingered to the fading strains of "I Love You Truly." Life for me oozed with the golden glow of wonder. Warmth and tender love. Deliriously happy at the fulfillment of a girlhood dream, I looked to the future.

The saddest moment that strangled my love and shattered my dreams was discovering our wonderful world had withered and died. Choked off with fear and worry, I moved mechanically through the pain of promise gone. Bouncing between fear and faith, I discovered depths I had not known. Reaching for a remedy for my reeling faith, I remembered the teaching of Dr. Donald Grey Barnhouse:

Nothing can touch us until it has passed

through the will of God. . . . We may have the absolute assurance that the plan of our own individual life has been fixed in God, that He is pursuing a definite purpose leading to a definite end, and that we may live in quiet assurance that all is well with us, even though we are passing through deep waters. . . .

To lay hold upon this fact is to calm the turbulence of life, and to bring quiet and confidence into the whole of the life. Nothing can touch me unless it passes through the will of God. God has a plan for my life. God is working according to a fixed, eternal purpose . . . each passing event of life is a part of the Father's plan. . . . As we look out upon our present circumstances we can be assured that we are exactly where our Father wishes us to be.[1]

Faith chased away the shadows of doubt. Peace displaced worry as I leaned upon these words of conviction. Struggling to believe that even my divorce was within the divine purpose of God, the

---

[1] Dr. Donald Grey Barnhouse, *Epistle to the Romans* (Philadelphia: © Donald Grey Barnhouse, 1954), pp. 24, 25, 26.

words of Dr. Barnhouse drew me back to the assurance of my belief. New understanding glanced off the written pages. Perspective. Over my rainbow, out of the dark clouds, His plan and purpose shined for me. Under the umbrella of His love, it became easier to accept that which before had felt totally unacceptable.

I also learned much through my job in those years. Under the duress of divorce, I had vibrated with panic at the pressures of a career. Emotionally unready for the demanding public, I was wisely advised that my personal problems would seem less troublesome as I interacted with people at work. Persisting in the pursuit of progress, I remained with the job. Valuing then the counsel of those currently more secure than I, in time I agreed. Wisdom existed in working. Involvement in a goal created a capacity for growth.

Employment was not new to me. Structured differently now, however, the responsibilities of my life engulfed me in numerous decisions. Commitments. Planning. All were *my* decisions. With much to learn, fawnlike, I sought to flee the glare of the financial game, impossible though that was. Securing my own credit, filing my income tax, managing my bills and purchases—all caused me to learn quickly. Forced to learn about money management, I timidly investigated investment possibilities. Sorting out the disastrous from the beneficial. Accepting what was realistic for my limited means.

My naivete' in business matters appalled me. Valuing the counsel of friends, I queried business associates for their expertise.

> In the multitude of counsellors there is safety. (Prov. 11:14)

Generous with time, eager in willingness, they discussed my opportunities and my alternatives. The guidance of those wiser than I fortified me with confidence when I reached the moment of commitment.

My housing required another decision. Should I remain in the beautiful home built by us such a few years before? Many dreams had gone into every brick and tile. Endless plans in modifying the design of the builder's model. Creative features and exciting colors, unique and personalized concepts culminating in a dazzling interior. The joy and satisfaction of living in this personalized product of our combined labor of love now pounded me with mixed feelings. I dwelt alone among the memories.

I wanted to stay, but the past was haunting me. To end the sparkling joy surging from fulfillment of years of dreams was traumatic. Camelot had come late and ended too abruptly. The light of that brief shining moment flickered, but had not gone out completely. Sharing my scintillating sentiments with a friend, I asked, "Because one has given up the dream, why should the other?"

Responding with a question, he asked, "What dream? It belonged to you both. It's gone."

Difficult as it was to accept, I finally acknowledged its truth. The house we created resulted from our shared dream. To live with the departed past left only illusion. Like bursting bubbles disintegrating in their dancing colors, so only fantasy could prefer the lonely mirage mirrored by my memories.

Deciding to depart was daring. A fresh start could be advantageous. Each step that removed me further from the painful past spelled progress.

Longing to avoid a mistake, I continued in search of God's direction. Evidence that would point me to His will. Relying on prayer, the Bible and various circumstances, I made the decision.

I believed it was time to go. A year and three months of living alone in my lovely Shangri-La proved to me it was possible. Now the time had come to discover the something of value existing in a new beginning. A for-sale sign went up.

I moved to an apartment, and in time the wisdom of my decision became apparent. Upon leaving the house of my dreams, I compensated for my loss by selecting a beautiful, spacious apartment. Years passed, and rents rose.

Ultimately I moved to a smaller apartment within the large apartment compound. A year and a half later, when the entire complex converted to condominiums, I discovered the significance of my earlier move. Current renters were allowed notable consideration in the purchase price of their unit. But could I manage even that? Seesawing between moving again or purchasing, I carefully weighed my options! I again sought the advice of business friends. Prayerfully, I searched for direction from God. My conviction grew. I *must* find a way to keep my apartment. Juggling my limited resources, I finally joined the condo parade! Looking back, I realized I could not have bought the larger unit. I thanked God for nudging me out to the smaller apartment but allowing me to remain within the complex. The wisdom of my decision has been constantly confirmed. Wisdom given, I believe, in response to my dependence on God. My seeking His will. Commitment to His leading.

During these years alone my experiences have encompassed the whispering winds of change. I have stood on the vistas of victory, and I have wandered in the void of the valleys. I have felt the transitoriness of time.

Five personal crises sent me to the hospital during the first six years following my divorce. Four resulted in surgery. Each time I was supported by the faithfulness of my son; he accompanied me and assisted as he could. His presence eased the frightening feelings of the unknown. Removed the dread of the obscure. These traumatic experiences were laced with lessons of faith. Trust in God's direction enhanced my faith and hedged me in to the security and serenity of His love.

There were also the happy times.

These included my first solo vacation. The experience of traveling alone is ordinary to many. But for me it was unique. My vacations had been many, but always with my husband. This solitary adventure required all the moxie I could muster! The initial chapter of charting the unknown, without my companion, called for courage! Bolstered in confidence and strengthened in self-assurance, this trip beckoned with adventure. Independence.

Fascinating Jamaica, the land of limbo dancers, was as exciting and undulating as the ocean. It was also as peaceful as the warm tropical sun or moon allowed.

The ride down the Rio Grande River from Port Antonio pulsated with the beauty of the island. Twenty-five-foot-long rafts made of bamboo poles were woven tightly together. The river man poling the raft between the steep banks explored the island's lush interior. I rode the raft alone, except for the guide, and softly sang the Keswick Doxology that welled up within!

> Praise God from whom all blessings flow;
> Praise Him, all creatures here below.
> Allelulia! Allelulia!
> Praise Him, above ye heavenly hosts—
> Praise Father, Son and Holy Ghost.
> Allelulia! Allelulia!
> Allelulia! Allelulia!
> Allelulia.[2]

I thrilled to the tantalizing beauty I beheld! I thanked God for my new freedom bringing me to this exciting adventure. I knew the mornings would be fresh with the spirit of the tropics.

It was a gentle day in the Caribbean. Early morning sounds, seductive in their softness, stirred among the silent trade winds. Glittering in the glare of the glorious sunlight was this sparkling jewel in the wonderful world of the tropics. Jamaica throbbed with spirit, with the beat of carefree enchantment.

---
[2]Thomas Ken, The Keswick Doxology.

I took a taxi from my hotel to an art gallery just outside the free port shops in the small village. Away from the main road and nestled deep in the lush tropical foliage, glistening with dew from the midnight rain, was a villa high above the ocean. A few yards away a studio housed the works of art I had come to see. None of the paintings shown captured the beauty, the enchantment, of this isle called Jamaica.

I left the gallery. My eyes were riveted to the far horizon past the sand beaches that were washed white by the crystal-clear Caribbean and rimmed by graceful palms under the canopy of azure skies. Whispering echoes of ocean waves drifted up to where I stood. From this high vantage point the sound of the sea and the sight of the unbelievable sky would be forever etched upon my mind. I wanted to stay. But, I had to believe rather that I would return again to the island paradise. My flight in fantasy to the foreign lands I'd read about as a child was being fulfilled.

My first vacation alone, vibrating with the joy of accomplishment and the thrill of adventure in the uncharted and unknown, promised delicious holidays ahead. Gratefully, I acknowledged the guidance of God and my sensitivity to His leading. I reveled in my awareness of His direction. I was learning to be me, for me.

Other areas of change in my life included dabbling in projects. The most challenging for me was an invention I designed. Discovering a new concept for a woman's handbag, it was conceived through frustration with current designs. Endeavoring to remove the irritating features of the old, I have constructed that which is functional, but is also designed with flair. Ending the fumbling inherent in existing construction, I envision my design to be a distinct aid to today's discriminating woman. Hours, dollars and dreams have surrounded the model now ready for presentation for potential marketing. Fascinating to create, I delighted in yet another avenue of self-expression.

My social life also changed as dating confronted me suddenly at my divorce. I remember the first man on this new dating scene.

He was tall and dark. Handsome, too, with an infectious smile and a contagious laugh. Inviting me to dinner, a different set of problems overshadowed the anticipated pleasure. Dating would be difficult.

My self-image was still that of wife and mother, and I was angry at the conflict I now felt. I longed to continue in the role I had known. With it I was comfortable. I did not then emotionally accept that my marriage had ended. I only knew intellectually that my divorce was a fact. It was to be a long time before I would feel single again. My feelings were confused. Out of a concern for my children, I hesitated to begin going out. What would they think? How would they react? Would they accept me in this new role? I was their *mother*. If I had an escort, it should be their father!

But this was *my* reaction! My feelings were a potpourri of dread and desire, misgivings and memories, fears and fantasies—all tinged with restlessness and resentment.

But I was also a woman with needs. If a man desired my company, why shouldn't I enjoy his companionship? I knew I needed no one's approval but my own. With apprehension, as that of a schoolgirl before her first prom, I accepted my first dinner date.

Quickly I discovered the dating game had changed. Attitudes were different. Standards seemed gone. Rules had disappeared. Yet, God had not erased His commandments. A wife of many years, I had been catapulted into the dating arena with less sophistication than the single woman who had been dating over the years. As my marital status had suddenly shifted, I saw the perils of singleness. I realized how threatening it was to one as vulnerable as I.

For the single woman to work out this segment of her life, it can be a devastating experience. Or a personal triumph. Enduring the turmoil of this test ferrets out the true grit of the woman. If she needs to prove her femininity, or if she finds it necessary to bolster her wounded ego via wine, men and music, she will fall prey to the many men who are eagerly waiting in the wings. If she comes to terms with this area of her life, in total commitment to God, her rewards will be many. She will maintain a respect for herself, while also realizing a new appreciation of her value to God.

> Know ye not that your body is the temple of the Holy Ghost which is in you, which ye have of God, and ye are not your own? For ye are bought with a price: therefore glorify God in your body, and in your spirit, which are God's. (1 Cor. 6:19, 20).

The woman who is genuinely free has a choice. Truly, she is—on her own.

5
Beyond Myself

Over the years I have become more keenly aware of God's method of accomplishing His purpose. That He works through people. Or things.

God could do anything. Everything. Without men. Or means. But that is not His way. The Bible illustrates this often. As in the story of Jesus feeding the multitude. With a little boy's lunch.

Wonder. Awe. Curiosity. All were mirrored in the small boy's face as he stared while his little lunch was given away one day. Eyes opened wide in surprise, he watched as the crowd of people sitting upon the grass were fed. Surprise and bewilderment were etched on his small features. He saw the food he had brought, little by little and crumb by crumb, multiply. Enough to feed everyone. Not understanding, he stood in stunned silence.

God worked a miracle that day when He used the two fish and the five loaves of bread brought by the little boy. Jesus could have performed this miracle without food. Without the small boy. But He chose those means to bring about His purpose. This is God's way.

On another occasion Jesus made clay and healed a man.

> When he had thus spoken, he spat on the ground, and made clay of the spittle, and he anointed the eyes of the blind man with the clay, And he said unto him, Go, wash in the pool of Siloam. . . . He went his way therefore, and washed, and came seeing. (John 9:6, 7)

Clay was the means Jesus used. He possessed the power to heal the man by a command. By a look. A touch. But He chose means: clay. And then He told the man to do something. In obeying, the man was healed.

When a king lay dying, God again performed a miracle. In the Old Testament, the healing of King Hezekiah is described. Near death, God promised,

> Behold, I will heal thee: . . . And I will add unto thy days fifteen years. . . . Take a lump of figs. And they took and laid it on the boil, and he recovered. (2 Kings 20:5-7)

God used the lump of figs as the means for healing King Hezekiah.

Within my life, I have experienced God using means to achieve His purpose. Methods to realize His plans.

One instance concerned my father. Another related to me. Each confirmed that God uses methods. Means.

It was in the year 1952 in a thriving midwestern city. My husband pastored a small church near the center of town. The ring of the telephone pierced the still of one warm spring evening. In the study, my husband picked up his phone as I simultaneously picked up the extension phone downstairs. No one was aware of my presence on the line as I listened in shocked silence. The message I heard reported the illness of my father. A brain tumor was suspected. After hearing the click of the phone and hanging up the receiver, I flung myself upon the bed, weeping unconsolably. I longed for my father. I needed to weep. My devoted collie, King, leaping upon the bed, whined as he licked my face and tugged at my hair.

My physician-father had seen others suffer. He had witnessed death. His own wish was to die quickly. Now those words, "brain tumor," haunted me. I envisioned a lengthy illness. A lingering death. Thinking of the pain for the one I loved, I was distraught. This was my father! A man who had brought healing to many. A country doctor who made house calls. Who did not refuse patients in the middle of the night. A beloved physician in one small community and its environs for over thirty-one years. He had served. Now he was the patient. He suffered.

I knew in my heart I would try for him. *How* I could help was yet obscure. Try I must. Determined to review the medical report, I knew I would investigate every possibility of hope. There *had* to be a way.

Soon afterwards I left for Chicago. My sister and I took my father's X-rays to his friend, then an official of a large Chicago hospital. Gravely studying the X-rays, he acknowledged only a slight possibility of a successful operation. He offered a thin ray of hope. Were it *his* X-ray, he would want the slight chance pursued.

Only my father could make that decision.

Clutching the X-rays and our faint promise of hope, we returned with aching hearts.

Confronting our father with the news and the possible alternative was traumatic for all. Naturally resistant, humanly hesitant and innately reluctant, the moment of decision descended upon him with the imminent dread of danger. I pleaded with a desperation born of love. We prayed with the hope of healing and the calm of commitment.

My father had a vibrant, vital faith,

> If ye have faith as a grain of mustard seed . . . nothing shall be impossible unto you. (Matt. 17:20)

> According to your faith be it unto you. (Matt. 9:29)

Arriving at a decision, he agreed to the operation. Pale and wan, he was wheeled into surgery. The burden of my persuasion weighed heavily upon me. My father's faith helped me then, as I trusted God as never before. My faith seemed small, but strong. The hope we had been given flickered in its smallness. But our trust in God overshadowed fear with a mighty strength. I prayed the prayer of Peter:

> Lord, I believe; help thou my unbelief. (Mark 9:24)

The major surgery lasted for seemingly endless hours. Struggling, we waited. Tension heightened as anguish gnawed, and agony churned inside me. Yet, assurance of the "everlasting arms" kindled a quiet strength that wrapped around my icy fear. It warmed me with its vigor and calmed me by nudging out my fright.

The surgeon, eventually appearing, intoned the welcome words that the operation was a success. Not only would my father survive, but the tumor had been located behind the eye. Away from the brain. It was not malignant. Its removal left no damage.

Punctuated with sobs, relief rolled over me as I allowed the words of the amazing report to penetrate my mesmerized mind. Overwhelmed with gratitude to God, no words could match my feelings. Faith had been rewarded. As humans, we had doubted. As Christians, our faith had been greater than our doubt. The suspense had ended. Relief replaced anguish. Gratefulness surged. Could we ever doubt again?

The surgeon's prognosis was that my father would perhaps live six or seven years following this critical surgery. But God was gracious. Following recuperation and with no physical impairment, he returned to his medical practice. He lived, as King Hezekiah of old, fifteen more years.

I will always cherish my father's words of gratitude pouring forth through his tears. Sensitive to his feelings and moved by his love, I listened to his words of wonder. Wonder wrought in the mind of God. His thin, almost invisible scar was ever a forceful and poignant testimony to me of the strength of his faith. The faith of others. And the power of Almighty God. Quivering, I choked and shuddered, reflecting on those high stakes—the day I trusted God for my father's life.

> This poor man cried, and the Lord heard him, and saved him out of all his troubles. (Ps. 34:6)

> The effectual fervent prayer of a righteous man availeth much. (James 5:16)

This experience in faith, echoing across the mountains and the valleys of time, moved along to my nightmarish days of separation. Standing alone in my divorce, I remembered. I remembered the faith of my father. And I remembered my own faith. Never again did I question that God uses means, whether people or things. He *could* have provided instant healing for my father. But He chose to use doctors, nurses and medicine.

As God chose means for my father then, He chose means for me following my divorce. God *could* have healed immediately my emotional wounds. But He chose to heal by a method. Not an instantaneous cure. But through a channel.

Hope for me came by means of a professional

counselor. God used him to help me heal my torn emotions. In his wisdom and support he provided the atmosphere in which I could face myself.

There is a time for tears and depression. There is a season for anger and rage. For sadness, loneliness and fear. God does not dehumanize us when we become Christians. We feel as deeply as before. Our passions are as intense. Our emotional hungers as real. We long. We yearn. We cry. We agonize. To deny ourselves the expression of these feelings is to deprive ourselves release essential to healing.

For me to express what I felt rather than what I thought was difficult. My feelings were guarded and protected. I knew what I thought, but needed someone's permission to give way to the seething, untamed anger. The desperate, hopeless sadness lurking within.

That Someone whose permission I sought, I believe, was God. I sensed a sinfulness in giving vent to the ugliness I felt. Emotional outbursts did not seem to conform to my concept of Christian conduct. Acknowledging that God knew my agony made it easier for me to ventilate my feelings. I discovered the value of expression, negative though it was. The dammed-up passions churned, breaking through in torrents of emotion, as I realized relief in release. Hours of trusting and sharing rolled on relentlessly and brought me to the heart of healing.

The perceptive therapist culled out that which was negative and destructive, as he preserved that which was positive and healthful. His insight and interpretation, his direction and patience, were vital in my coming to feel less afraid. Under his guidance, I brought together the polarized areas of my life; the fears and the faiths, the stresses and the strengths.

This brilliant, yet sensitive analyst was the catalyst used by God to help me find my own place in the sun. His impact, as I was discovering my inner resources of courage and resiliency, was an integral force in this process of my becoming. He was the means used by God for my recovery. For the road back from emotional crisis.

My progress was steady, but slow. I compared therapy to cutting off a dog's tail inch by inch. It hurt. The pain was protracted. Prolonged. One step backward for each two forward.

Someone has said, the glory is not in never falling, but in rising every time you fall.

Trial and error, weakness and strength, failure and success, were carving out a pattern. In the midst of my vulnerability I sensed the growing awareness that I *would* survive.

Often there were setbacks. Joy in my new-found strength was stomped out, as fragile flowers beneath the crush of heavy marching boots. A sudden crisis, a fresh trial, could spin me back into the isolated aloneness from which I sought escape. Many times my discouragement and perceived defeat seemed overwhelming. Reckless in my resolve to reap the reward of my tortuous route through therapy, I was disillusioned and discouraged at the temporary reversals. The detours in my partial defeat. The disillusionment in delay.

I felt unable to follow through in this painful process. I sensed my need to escape the hurt. To cover my eyes and close my ears to the truth. To the distasteful. Analysis was tedious. Trying. Terrifying. I pondered if I had reinforced my habits for too long a time to change. But I would not let myself fail. Convinced it was up to me, the challenge to help myself became a driving force. A persuasive motivation.

Dr. Carl Rogers writes:

> This process of the good life is not, I am convinced, a life for the faint hearted. It involves the stretching and growing of becoming more and more of one's potentialities. It involves the courage to be. It means launching oneself fully into the stream of life. Yet the deeply exciting thing about human beings is that when the individual is inwardly free, he chooses

as the good life this process of becoming.[1]

The courage to be! My courage seemed so small. Often I questioned if I possessed any at all. Gradually, beneath my fear, I discovered that quality which I treasured. It was little, but mighty. It was a tiny diamond of dynamite. Call it fearlessness. Call it bravery. Or valor. By whatever name, the feeling was the same! The fact that it existed could not be denied. Somehow, through the divine alchemy this small facet of fearlessness was being transformed into something precious. Something called courage: the courage to be.

Courage forced me to see this therapy through. A day finally came when I could say to my therapist, "I don't need you any more. I'm strong enough to go it alone." The mosaic of my life, woven of the anguish and the pain of the past, the uncertainty of today, and the hope of tomorrow, was taking on more constructive form and design.

Back in the summer of 1968, my husband and I had attended the Forest Home Bible Conference in the beautiful San Bernardino Mountains near Redlands, California. The setting was peaceful. The atmosphere relaxing. The speakers were stimulating, and one message confronted us with the observa-

---
[1] Carl R. Rogers, Ph.D., *On Becoming a Person* (Boston: Houghton Mifflin Co., 1961), p. 196.

tion, "It is the set of the sail that counts! Are you heading in the right direction?" Not profound, but provocative.

What *was* right? Right for me? How could I know? I accepted the Bible as my guide. My rule of faith and practice. I trusted God to lead me in inner conviction. I had experienced it *is* possible to know the right direction. Little things God used as indicators. Larger, more significant circumstances reaffirmed my convictions. Verses of Scripture leaped into mind. Exploding with confirmation. Support.

> Call unto me, and I will answer thee, and shew thee great and mighty things, which thou knowest not. (Jer. 33:3)

Now, in my life alone, I sought to be going in the right direction. At times I wandered, lost in the turnbacks and detours. Confused in *my* way that had become clouded. But God, in patience and love, signaled His direction. Gently, very gently, He drew me back. And, in drawing me back to himself, He moved me—beyond myself. What we actually are is a gift to us from God. But what we each make of ourselves, what we develop from our potential, is our offering to Him. Our gift to Him. This process of becoming was providing my gift for God.

6

Into the Future—Unafraid

As the far side of dawn was foreboding, the near side beckoned as a place of beauty. The closer I came to the newness of dawn, the more brilliant the rays of hope. The freshness of a new day.

I began to enjoy life again. I discovered a new vitality, born of an inner trust. A basic belief. This vitality, projecting itself on the screen of my shattered life, assured me that pieces can fit together. Energy so long spent in fighting my inner battle was at last being freed for purposeful living. Freed for creating something better. I was building. Building on the trust and courage I had come to know and value. Proving that His strength is adequate. His support is sufficient. This crisis experience of my divorce was giving me a second chance at my life.

Anne Morrow Lindbergh wrote:

> The good past is so far away and the near past is so horrible, and the future is so

perilous... perhaps we never appreciate the here and now until it is challenged.[1]

I knew I was being challenged. The unknown, the untried tomorrow, had become today. The other side of indecision and insecurity was filled with promise. Freedom. I sensed being on the edge of adventure. The feeling at my divorce as "half of a pair of scissors" was fading. Strength was moving me forward to the exhilarating feeling of a new person. A wife for many years, it was frightening when first forced free. Then, feeling abandoned, I had almost succumbed in a sea of uncertainty.

Now I discovered there existed adventure in freedom. No longer did I wait for someone stronger than I, referred to by Dr. Erich Fromm as "the magic helper":

> One hopes to get everything one expects from life, from the magic helper, instead of by one's own actions.[2]

Limping along with small steps of risks in life, I was learning that each step forward led to greater trust in God. And in myself. In truth they were not

---
[1] Anne Morrow Lindbergh, *Gift from the Sea* (New York: Pantheon Books, Inc., 1955), pp. 126, 127.
[2] Erich Fromm, *Escape from Freedom* (New York: Rinehart and Company, Inc., 1941), p. 176.

INTO THE FUTURE—UNAFRAID

risks at all, but steps of faith, climbing to confidence through commitment. Little by little, as line upon line an architect pencils his design, I was drafting my own blueprint. Shadowing the master plan of God for my individual life.

My faith flourished as I no longer reached out for another stronger person. The strength pitching me forward grew from my own deep inner resources. In emotionally supporting myself I was creating my own harmony of life. Dr. Maxwell Maltz observes:

> Another person may like you, may even go out of his way to help you in a crisis, but he cannot live for you. He cannot make your decisions, cannot participate completely in your joys and heartbreaks; more, he cannot give you the capacity for success or failure, for self acceptance or self rejection.
>
> Your self image can give you this capacity. It can give you a sense of certainty as you live . . . the conviction that . . . you will support yourself. . . .
>
> When you are sure of this internal cushion

in crisis, then you know how to be certain in this uncertain world.[3]

This sense of certainty from my own self-image fused with my Christian faith. God was the One who had given me the ability to believe in Him for salvation. My faith was His gift.

> For by grace are ye saved through faith; and that not of yourselves: it is the gift of God: Not of works, lest any man should boast. (Eph. 2:8, 9)

Likewise, He gave me the capacity to believe in myself. To affirm me. My self-image. To create a life fulfilling for me. And pleasing to Him. This ability to support myself emotionally came from God. My part was to believe it, and to develop my God-given inner resources. Becoming more of the complete person God meant for me to be. His provision for growth is available. He promises strength.

> My grace is sufficient for thee: for my strength is made perfect in weakness. (2 Cor. 12:9)

He invites belief:

---
[3]Maxwell Maltz, M.D., F.I.C.S., *Creative Living for Today* (New York: Trident Press, 1967), p. 12.

INTO THE FUTURE—UNAFRAID

> I have prayed for thee, that thy faith fail not. (Luke 22:32)

He provides freedom:

> If the Son therefore shall make you free, ye shall be free indeed. (John 8:36)

He longs for men to love:

> He that loveth not knoweth not God; for God is love. (1 John 4:8)

God's provision is for an integrated, whole individual—body, soul and spirit.

He promised abundant life. He said that in knowing Him, the Truth, we would be free. I had been freed from the guilt of sin. In a vertical dimension, as relating to my Creator, I was a Christian. On a horizontal level, in my self-actualization, I was free to be me. Free to discover who I am as a person. Free, as a single adult. Alone. More fully aware of my own identity. Apart from anyone else. Accepting myself. I was bringing order out of the chaos of a broken marriage and the tragedy of divorce. I was experiencing change.

Dr. Carl Rogers writes:

> When I accept myself as I am, then I

change . . . we cannot change, we cannot move away from what we are, until we thoroughly *accept* what we are. Then change seems to come about almost unnoticed.[4]

I found reward in getting close to others. I came to value moving toward another. I had healed enough to be able to give again. I found joy in losing myself as my own life touched others. Concern for another is what really matters. Reaching out initially to say, "I care." Growing in relationships, I found others. And I found more of myself. I was allowing myself to come near in genuine relating. Opening myself to rejection as well as to acceptance and love. But how fragile were my feelings!

I realized anew one of the reasons for our hesitating to form close relationships. If we share our innermost selves—who we really are—and if we then are disliked, we risk losing. Losing the relationship which we have desired. For we have shared. Given. And we then have no more to give.

This, perhaps more than any other reason, restrains us from openness. We lock out communication from fear that we will be rejected. We are afraid we will walk emotionally naked, stripped of

---
[4]Carl R. Rogers, Ph. D., *On Becoming a Person* (Boston: Houghton Mifflin Co., 1961), p. 17.

all we are in ourselves.

This fear inhibits us, and we relate to others on a superficial level. From surface feelings. Few are the persons with whom we feel free. Free enough to confide anything. Anything! But, if we are free, we do have a choice. A choice to share ourselves, or to withhold. But, if we feel free to withhold, do we also feel free to share?

Anne Morrow Lindbergh writes:

> We have so little faith in the ebb and flow of life, of love, of relationships. We leap at the flow of the tide, and resist in terror its ebb. We are afraid it will never return. We insist on permanency, on duration, on continuity; when the only continuity possible, in life as in love, is in growth, in fluidity—in freedom.[5]

It was becoming easier for me not to look back. Life was sparkling once more, as I was feeling again the joy of living. I was making progress. Not in giant leaps, but by small steps. Very small steps. Over a long period of time. My dependence on God is expressed by Dr. Peter Marshall:

Thou hast invited me "to ask, to seek, to

---
[5] Anne Morrow Lindbergh, *Gift from the Sea* (New York: Pantheon Books, Inc., 1955), p. 108.

knock," assuring me that if I ask, it shall be given unto me; if I seek, I shall find; if I knock, it shall be opened unto me.

Help me to believe that, O God. Give me the faith to ask, knowing that I shall receive. Give me the faith to seek, believing that I shall surely find. Give me the faith and the persistence to knock, knowing that it shall be indeed opened unto me.

Help me to live the Christian life in daring faith and humble trust, that there may be worked out in me, even in me, Thy righteousness and goodness. With a sense of adventure, I make this prayer. Amen.[6]

My constant prayer had been for direction in my life. I did not connect this prayer with a certain dream. A dream that kept recurring. I saw in my dream a fork in the road. Always I visited the same area. Vivid and lucid, it was enough for me to realize I returned in my dream to the same place. The identical site. I drew a map of what I saw in this repeated dream. But its interpretation remained a mystery. Puzzled and intrigued by my

---
[6]*The Prayers of Peter Marshall*, copyright © 1954 by Catherine Marshall. Published by Chosen Books, Lincoln, Virginia. Used by permission.

INTO THE FUTURE—UNAFRAID

dreams, I often sought to decode them. I was amazed and amused by the interpretations I came upon, though sometimes I found them frightening! This particular dream perplexed me. Until the following summer. After returning from my vacation, the meaning of the dream became clear. I understood.

The vacation that opened for me the meaning of my dream had been in the Colorado Rockies. I had returned to a spot originally visited in 1967. The beauty and grandeur of the massive purple peaks towered above the quiet valley below. The crisp, dry air and stillness amidst the whispering pines convinced me that this is where I wished to retire.

Going back now to a place I had visited while married was deeply significant to me. I had consciously avoided returning to places of the past. The memories, I sensed, would rob me of the pleasure I now sought. Recollections of the past could be painful. Revisiting now a place of happy former experiences proved exciting evidence of my progress. I had overcome another hurdle. Conquered one more obstacle in this slow process of becoming. Nine years had passed since my divorce before I was able to face the past without a problem and revisit where I had been in happier times.

Currently it was the summer of 1978. I longed for the ministry of the mountains. Their solemnity. I knew the quiet would give perspective.

> Be still, and know that I am God. (Ps. 46:10)

The hush would calm and caress with comfort. Stillness prods us to listen to the quiet.

> I will lift up mine eyes unto the hills, from whence cometh my help. My help cometh from the Lord, which made heaven and earth. (Ps. 121:1-2)

In the heart of the Rockies, three hours southwest of both Denver and Colorado Springs, lies the small town of Buena Vista. Beyond is Trail West Lodge. A family lodge, built in the sixties, it is an unusual one-of-a-kind place. Situated in spectacular scenery, it is more than just a beautiful place. It provides a vacation with a purpose. Trail West is owned and operated by Young Life, a national interdenominational organization reaching out to young people. The lodge exposes adults to the many aspects of Young Life's Ministry. It affords, in a low-key approach, an opportunity to encounter the attractiveness of Christ.

It was to this spot that I returned in the summer of 1978. As exciting as my successful return to a place of former happier days was the revelation of the meaning of my recurring dream! High in the mountains, amidst 14,000-foot peaks, I saw the same mountain roads I had traveled so often in my dream! The identical curves and bends, the turns and cutbacks, the same peaks and rugged terrain. I was being allowed to live my dream!

Then came the insight. The sudden realization. I understood the reason I had come west. I knew why God had directed me to Colorado and Young Life's Trail West. I understood my dream: the fork-in-the-road was in the mountains!

In life, I was facing a crucial decision. I had a choice to make. The fork in the road I had stood at so often in my dreams was literally here in the mountains. I could not take both roads. This time it was for real. It was up to me. I met God anew in this place of His appointment. The guidance had been given in answer to my prayer. Now the decision was mine to make. The gray areas, the undefined dimensions of life, came under the scrutiny of God, and I chose to acknowledge His Lordship in all areas of my life.

> I the Lord search the heart, I try the reins, even to give every man according to his ways, and according to the fruit of his doings. (Jer. 17:10)

I felt release in commitment. Relief in surrender. Peace in abandonment to His claims. Captive by His love.

Make me a captive, Lord
And then I shall be free.
Force me to render up my sword,
And I shall conqueror be.
I sink in life's alarms
When by myself I stand.
Imprison me within thine arms,
And strong shall be my hand.

My will is not my own
Till thou has made it Thine.
If it wants to reach a monarch's Throne,
It must its crown resign.
It only stands unbent
Amid the clashing strife.
When on thy bosom
It has leant
And found in thee its life.[7]

In Christ I was born to be free. Freedom from the slavery to self allowed me to make my choices. To choose the higher good. The ministry of the Mountains had surfaced once more. And, significantly, I did not dream that same dream again.

In quiet confidence I moved into the future—unafraid!

---

[7]George Matheson, "Make Me A Captive, Lord."

7
Touching Tomorrow

The mourning that followed my divorce was ending. Mourning follows loss, and the death of a marriage occasions loss. Its awareness may be masked in part or in whole. Unlike in the presence of physical death, a divorced person may not even grieve over the departed spouse. Some feel a sense of relief. Others celebrate the new detachment with apparent joy. Reveling in their freedom.

But inevitably the loss of one once cherished more than any other causes a feeling of emptiness. A touch of wistfulness lingers, as a special person has moved out of one's life. Someone once treasured is no longer reachable. Suddenly the missing moments of shared experiences telescope with memories. Memories that rekindle passions of the past. Bitter or bittersweet. The dissolution of the close tie and the intimate bond of marriage inevitably leaves a sense of sorrow. Varying in degree.

These feelings are not always recognized as loss. There are those who cannot acknowledge their formless feelings. Others deny such responses exist. Many reject their honest emotions, relabeling them.

The realization of a void may surface at once. Suddenly. Or it may be only in time that feelings are owned and allowed the expression they need. For me, the awareness was sudden. As the curtain falling at the close of a play. The era had ended. Realization that our union was broken immediately came crashing at my feet, as a fragile ornament tumbling from atop a Christmas tree. My shattered feelings surfaced immediately.

Each of us has his own timetable of emotional reaction that determines the speed of healing. It is a process. There is no instant recovery from loss. With his own unique personality, coming from his individual background, each discovers—in time—a diminishing of that loss.

How rapidly pain diminishes depends, in part, on the degree of hurt one has experienced. Of trauma that has been felt. Raw emotions and bruised hearts heal in proportion to our ability to express ourselves. Time is the healing catalyst. For me, as time crept forward, it edged out pain. Ushering in a degree of peace.

Time.

A friend of mine whose daughter had just died wrote me out of her sorrow and grieving:

> Time is something I can't explain. It just doesn't exist at times, and it stands still at times, and nothing matters at times. Time? What is time when in such deep sorrow? Time that sometimes doesn't seem to exist, or matter.

I felt the ache in each throbbing word that was riddled with pain. My awareness of her strength and courage only emphasized this depth of need she now expressed. For her, time just did not matter. As I tried to write, words would not come. I longed to help, but I cannot explain time.

I can only try to understand the one in need. I can remember the pain of those poignant moments when loss made me reel. When sorrow sealed me into my own world of hurt. And sadness snuggled deep in the dark corners of my life.

In remembering, I can say in as many ways as possible, I care. In showing I care, others become brave enough to trust me with their feelings. I can show that I share someone else's sorrow. I can assure that I am praying. I can communicate often. Listen. Empathize. Try to be supportive in understanding. I can show love in every way God brings to mind. The little things. A phone call. A letter. A smile. A touch. I can witness to God's adequacy in my life. I can share the value of time. For time heals. Time puts things in perspective. I remember an illustration used by Dr. Barnhouse.

The first time I met him was when my husband and I arrived in Philadelphia in 1940. Strangers in the city, it was a Wednesday evening that we visited the Tenth Presbyterian Church, of which Dr. Barnhouse was the pastor. Rarely was he in his pulpit during the week, due to his conference ministry. However, in the plan of God, this man who was to influence our lives in such a singular way conducted his own service that particular weeknight. Introducing ourselves at the conclusion of the service, a new friendship was begun. Soon afterwards we joined his church, and over the years we spent many hours with him discussing the Bible.

We attended Dr. Barnhouse's own Bible Conference in Mt. Gretna, Pennsylvania, one year, and on Sunday he invited us to join him in the return to Philadelphia for the evening service at his church. During the drive, he offered to preach that evening upon anything we would request! Surprised by this generous offer, we began sharing our concerns.

That evening we were privileged to listen to a sermon that had been prepared for us specifically. While en route to church! Though thirty years have passed, I recall the sermon and the colorful illustration around which he built his message.

He referred to the little chapel in Paris, France, Sainte Chapelle. Built in 1246-1248, of Gothic architecture, it is a stone-vaulted church of a series of slim, heavily buttressed piers, supporting a soaring vault. The high tracery windows, slim and jeweled, are of brilliant glass which is largely red and blue. The purple light that streams through infuses a magic beauty with its incredibly warm and bright effect.

Dr. Barnhouse described how one approaches the old structure. Having heard of its majestic beauty, one does not find it so immediately. His eyes are still blinded by the sun outside, from whence he has come. Only in waiting until his eyes clear and adjust to the inside does he experience the awesome beauty of this little jewel! If he were to return immediately from where he entered, his eyes would still be blinded. It is the waiting. The *time*. The adjusting. The adapting to the new environment. The different atmosphere. The soft glow of the sanctuary in contrast to the brilliant sunlight on the outside. Only after allowing time for the adjustment can one behold the awesome beauty and quiet majesty that surrounds him. The lesson is superb, illustrating the ministry of time.

Time makes the difference. Time mellows. Time gives perspective. Time? Does it matter? Perhaps only as we allow it to matter. Only as we permit it to be used in healing our broken hearts. Only as we make significant use of it. As we make time work for us.

For me, I discovered that only as I experienced time did I adjust to my circumstances. Only as I was aware of my new situation could I adapt to it. Only as I allowed time for the tears to flow and the mist to leave did I begin to appreciate the shifting opportunity. The wonder of God's planned purpose for me. I reached out and touched tomorrow.

My loss was being felt less. My sensation of slippage was shifting. There were many reasons responsible for my growth.

My commitment to God and my trust in His love, parachutelike, bore me above disaster and defeat.

The professional help I had the courage to seek stabilized my base for growth.

My mother ministered in measures of love and devotion. I recall her shock when I shared with her the turmoil of my marriage. Her hurt and pain obvious, she was the one who opened her arms and her home to me when the separation came. Ready to help, she gave of herself when my pain was greatest. She loved when life for me was loss. She understood when compassion was my desperate need.

My children supported me with love and tender

concern. Since each of us comes into this world with one biological mother and father, to expect a child of any age to "take sides" is cruel. It asks more than anyone has the right to ask. I am thankful God gave me the wisdom to ask for nothing. I am also grateful for their love that surrounded me. Their comfort fell over me as a heavy silent snow. Their support became my bridge to freedom. It was my son who accompanied me to church after the divorce hearing. Sharing in my sorrow and communicating his strength, his presence cushioned the pain.

In my own determination to get up when I fell and try to walk again, I was grinding out my own path to overcoming. Healing. I was discovering that tragedy lies not in falling, but in failing to get up. In failing to try again. And again. I was learning it is acutely painful, but definitely possible, to go through the night of darkness and the midnight of despair to finally see the other side: this side of dawn.

Reading rewarded me in this reconstruction period. Reaching for help, I uncovered gems of thought and germs of truth that smoothed the way to coping. And beyond. Insights of writers, psychologists and theologians meshed with the inspiration of poets. Authors, new or renowned, caused me to think for myself. Inspiration and enrichment, as wave upon wave, surged in my continuous movement and growth. I revisualized my potential. I felt a degree of success. I valued these new feelings about myself. I treasured the progress I had made.

The ministry of music uplifted me more than I could have dreamed. In brushing by the hurts and glancing past the pain, it brought calm while I listened. Exhilaration as I participated. The inspiration of music molded my attitudes, moving me toward new motivation.

I recall the evenings beside the fireplace in the large family room of our home, when my two small granddaughters and I curled cozily in the rocker. I joined the children in singing their little childhood medleys. The song most often requested was the childhood favorite:

> Jesus loves me this I know:
> For the Bible tells me so!
> Little ones to Him belong,
> They are weak, but He is strong.
>
> Yes, Jesus loves me!
> Yes, Jesus loves me!
> Yes, Jesus loves me!
> The Bible tells me so.[1]

---

[1] From *Little Christian's Songbook*, compiled by Daniel R. Burow and Carol Greene. © 1975 by Concordia Publishing House. Used by permission.

TOUCHING TOMORROW

As the years passed and the children have grown, I still find for myself in that little song the antidote to worry. I have found it impossible for me to remain sad while singing that simple melody. When driving along in the car, if discouraged, lonely or distressed, I often sing aloud this little song. Quickly, I sense my shift in mood as the simple, yet profound message sweeps me along to new assurance. Overwhelmed by the depth and vastness of God's love.

One song rose above all others in helping to heal my wounds, inspiring me as it has countless others. The lyrics erased despair and disillusionment, discouragement and defeat, as the melody swelled into a crescendo of triumph.

> Because He lives I can face tomorrow;
> Because He lives all fear is gone;
> Because I know He holds the future.
> And life is worth the living just because
>   He lives![2]

It is because He lives that I had courage to anticipate tomorrow. The assurance that Jesus Christ is alive wiped away my fear of the present. Or dread of the future. The knowledge that He

---

[2] *Because He Lives* by William J. and Gloria Gaither, copyright © 1971 by William J. Gaither. Used By Permission.

lives brought me security. Courage to cope. To hope. To live.

With the sounds of sacred music, this inspiring musical expression rose above and beyond to strengthen. Encourage. Enrich. Projecting the heart of the gospel, this song swelled within to alter my thinking. Change my feeling. Transform my day. As the strains of the lilting refrain lingered in my mind, the message heralded hope for what is "out there." That of which I had been apprehensive and afraid became the focus of anticipation and expectation. What I had feared was replaced by my faith in the future. Just because He lives!

Writing, having already carved its own creative corner in my new world of constructive change, continued to be therapeutic. Seldom did I reread my writing. The release in penning my reflections usually served its purpose. Flowing from my feelings six weeks after my divorce, however, I wrote:

> So life is to be lived—
> The how
> For me to find.
> The where
> Within myself
> Where all the answers lie.
>
> Ah! To see

Beyond the cobwebs
Spun of fear—and loss,
Of pain—and promise gone.

To find
The route
That I must take
Oh, precious pearl
I must make!

To know
Beyond doubts' long shadows,
To feel—
The questing cease—
To be—
In the sun of certainty
"I can" become "I am."

Ten years later I reaffirm what I wrote then. Time echoes its corroboration. The answers are all within. There exists no book with instant cures. There lies no magic within a cloistered club to sweep us to success. We each have just ourselves. And, if we dare, with the key of honesty we can unlock our future as well as our past. The trek through the jungle of self is individual. Being unique, only each one can carve his own path to individual potential.

Nestled around my mistakes and sorrows, I found my route. Woven of joys and victories, I felt the searching lessen. I have known the questing cease. I realize now a degree of certainty.

Given by my daughter a small charm for my bracelet, the size of a dime, it was inscribed with the words, "I can." Her belief in my strength and her confidence in my courage claimed an integral part in the positive phase of my struggle.

I climbed my mountain of misery until I reached the pinnacle of promise and hope. "I can" has become "I am." I am aware of being me. A person worthy of being. Unique and individual. Secure in my apartness. Aware of being capable of managing myself. I realize, in my progress, a degree of success far beyond my valley of fears and shadows. And serenity, as I touch tomorrow.

8
Morning and Joie de Vivre

In his sermon "The Problem of Falling Rocks," Dr. Peter Marshall wrote:

> I think the Christian treatment of trouble is splendidly illustrated by the oyster, into whose shell one day there comes a tiny grain of sand.
>
> By some strange circumstance, this tiny piece of quartz has entered into the shell of the oyster and there like an alien thing
>   an intruder
>   a cruel, unfeeling catastrophe
> imposes pain
>   distress
>   and presents a very real problem.
> What shall the oyster do?
>
> Well, there are several courses open . . .
>
>   . . . the oyster recognizes the presence of

the grim intruder, and right away begins to do something.
Slowly and patiently, with infinite care, the oyster builds upon the grain of sand—layer upon layer of a plastic, milky substance that covers each sharp corner and coats every cutting edge . . .
    and gradually . . . slowly . . .
        by and by a pearl is made . . .
            a thing of wondrous beauty
                wrapped around trouble.

The oyster has learned—by the will of God—to turn grains of sand into pearls
    cruel misfortunes into blessings . . .
        pain and distress into beauty.

And that is the lesson that we are to learn along this pilgrim way. The grace of God, which is sufficient, will enable us to make of our troubles the pearls they can become.[1]

The milky substance that wraps around the irritant is the waste of the oyster. In life, it is our unseemly side. That which we would disown. But

---
[1] Peter Marshall, *Mr. Jones, Meet the Master* (New York: Fleming H. Revell Co., 1949, 1950), pp. 172, 174, 175.

God uses. Just as He uses the oyster's waste to make the pearl. Our failures, fears, weaknesses, sins, ugliness, lack of faith, angers and frustrations all become that of which the pearl is made. God, in perfect synchronization, transforms our minuses into a thing of beauty.

My divorce, with its pain and suffering, with its sins and sorrows, was a grain of sand. But in the process of becoming, God was bringing forth ultimate beauty and loveliness. The tragedy of my divorce was being turned into blessing. The destruction redesigned into beauty. The pearl was in the process of becoming. It always will be.

Does the lesson of the oyster help in healing? Can it calm in crisis? It helped in reassuring me that God was making a thing of beauty out of my imperfections. It calmed, as I accepted that God pardons and forgives sins:

> I will forgive their iniquity, and I will remember their sin no more. (Jer. 31:34)

And, He also makes it possible for each of us to forgive ourselves.

Since all our thoughts and actions become a part of us forever, they affect us consciously or unconsciously. Awareness of present and memories of past guilt can be overwhelming—apart from His forgiveness of us. And our forgiveness of ourselves. Out of the ashes and rubble of our defeat, we can forgive. Ourselves. We can be assured that what was not in the perfect, directive will of God is now being turned into a thing of beauty.

In His patience He has permitted us to conceive our own plans, nurse our pride and prejudices, and release our passions. In divine metamorphosis He uses what we bring: these grains of sand. Being forgiven by Him, and having forgiven ourselves, we find peace. God and man, working together, willing and doing, create the eternal and enduring pearl of great price.

> He which hath begun a good work in you will perform it until the day of Jesus Christ. (Phil. 1:6)

My nightmare of divorce is over. The serenity of my life in the sun is more to be felt than analyzed. Perhaps a degree of disillusionment will always remain. A touch of wistfulness at the thought of what once was. The remembrance of my wedding date. A family photograph. A place we visited together. An unexpected dream. All part of the pattern of life.

I have asked myself, if God guides, did He direct me into a marriage which was a mistake? No, I believe God intended my husband and I to marry and share the life we lived those many years. I recall my calm deliberation in search of God's will, prior to my commitment to marriage. I believe now, as then, that it was His will for me to marry. When I did. And whom I did.

The man I married contributed to me as a person. Even as I did to him. In the process of becoming we each had a definitive part in the growth of the other. All that we brought, the positive and the negative, the helpful and that which had to be unlearned, has become a part of the persons we now are. Dr. Ernest White writes:

> Every thought, word and act has its consequences. What we are today depends largely on what we did yesterday and in all the preceding days, and what we think and how we act today decides what we shall be tomorrow. We cannot escape the consequences of the past.[2]

In committing myself to another in marriage I took a risk, as anyone does. In part, I lost. But one never loses completely, if he makes the grains of sand into pearls. I also gained, in part. I am happier

---
[2] Ernest White, M.B., B.S., *The Way of Release: For Souls in Conflict* (Fort Washington, Pa.: Christian Literature Crusade, 1947, 1956, 1960), pp. 90, 91.

for having loved and lost—to whatever degree I did lose. The paradox we live, that we can find happiness even in losing, is acceptable when viewed in the light of His love.

Helen Keller said:

> What we have once enjoyed we can never lose. . . . All that we love deeply becomes a part of us.[3]

I see the dark and the shadows as the other side of God's love. This other side is more difficult to comprehend, often being obscured by lack of faith. I look to what good has been, and I believe is yet to come. Dr. John Claypool has written:

> The one from whom had come the good old days, could be trusted to provide "good new days." If yesterday was so full of meaning, why not tomorrow? All the days come from the same source![4]

In writing this book, there is also an element of serendipity. Enjoyable things I didn't anticipate have been added to my life. New friends have been

---
[3]Helen Keller, *We Bereaved* (New York: Leslie Fulenwider, Inc., 1929), p. 2.
[4]John R. Claypool, *Tracks of a Fellow Struggler* (Waco, Tex.: *Word Books*, Publisher, 1974), p. 96. Used by permission of the publisher.

made. Friends of long standing find intrigue in my writing a book! They question me concerning it. Thereby this manuscript has become a vehicle for witnessing to my faith. A dimension has been added as I grow and change.

As discouragement diminishes, and the sense of loss fades, this current thrust of writing is chiseling out for me another opportunity in self-fulfillment. I am rewarded by inner contentment and satisfaction. As I make myself happy, I enrich my relationship with others. Cherished friendships are bound to follow.

Still another challenge has crept into my life. After ten years in one job, I grew restless. I sensed the need for change. That it was time to move on. Sometimes to move up, one must move on. In slow contemplation, and decisive commitment, I was receptive when God intervened.

Swiftly, in three consecutive days, three referrals confronted me with the identical opportunity. Forging ahead, I followed what I believed to be God's direction. Previous attempts at a change in jobs had aborted abruptly, leaving me confused and puzzled. Now, moving in confidence, I braved the interview. Considered the new opportunity. For I sought to carve out a new career.

The phone call offering me the job for which I had interviewed left me ecstatic! Stimulation at the thought of an exciting new life style—from the suburbs to the heart of the city—was exhilarating! However, I was also realistic.

Confident in my present position, the new opportunity required skills I must learn. Alongside challenge was apprehension, blunting my enthusiasm. I now was caught up in more prayer, deliberation and the search for guidance. In an unexpected moment my answer was to come.

It was early morning. Between bends and stretches of my daily exercise routine, I stopped abruptly. With fingers touching my toes, while breathing in short gasps, the words of Scripture burst into mind:

> I have set before thee an open door.
> (Rev. 3:8)

Straightening up, I paused and savored my confidence from this signal to go ahead! Move on. Up. It all seemed so clear. With verve I accepted my new opportunity!

Beginning in confidence I soon realized the old familiar panic button was close at hand! The specter of fear again stalked amid the uncertainty facing me in my sudden new challenge. Going from the known to the unknown, there existed my own familiar bridge of fear.

Stumbling across a yellowed piece of paper in

my father's old desk, I found several Bible verses scrawled in his handwriting. Special to him. One was to become a favorite of mine:

> Be strong and of a good courage; be not afraid, neither be thou dismayed: for the Lord thy God is with thee withersoever thou goest. (Josh. 1:9)

Lodging in my memory, I recalled it often during the difficult adjustment period of learning my new job. I remembered my past lessons that led to more intensely practicing the presence of Christ. Bringing to mind former successful experiences reawakened the dormant seeds of confidence that had grown strong in the past. Bottling those successes, and uncorking them at the appropriate moments, I began to wipe out the insecurity with which I now was grappling.

I also remembered a painting that had hung on the wall of my parental home. By the artist Phil Saint, it is entitled "The Way of the Cross Leads Home." In vivid colors and sweeping strokes, Mr. Saint dramatically depicts the empty cross of Christ as the bridge leading from this life to the next. Stretching horizontally it spans the shores from earth to beyond. Biblical details, brilliantly etched, portray the stream of humanity in their respective abodes. Reminded of the painting and the story it depicts, I realized that as the cross is the bridge from this life to the next, it is also the bridge from the security of here and now: the known, as we move to the unknown. From certainty to uncertainty. From assurance to the unsettled steps in our growth and progress.

Disappointed that I was unable to ride the crest of confidence acquired over the years in my previous job, I pondered in reflection. Reminding myself that God had set before me this open door, I believed He expected me to move on through it. And God never asks of us more than we are able. Awakening one Sunday morning, I recalled the verse:

> For God hath not given us the spirit of fear; but of power and of love, and of a sound mind. (2 Tim. 1:7)

Fear does not originate with God! I knew it was not His plan that I be frightened, whatever the circumstance. I also believed that fear could be overcome. It is His presence that countermands fear. That makes it possible to move from fear to faith.

On the same Sunday morning that I awakened with the Bible verse tripping through my foggy mind, the minister began his sermon by quoting the same verse for his text. His quotation was from another version:

> For God did not give us a spirit of timidity but a spirit of power and love and self-control. (2 Tim. 1:7)[5]

I was learning that the bridge from the known to the unknown can be frightening or freeing. I could climb from fear to freedom by the courage God provides. By the presence that removes dread. Foreboding. Apprehension. It is God that makes the difference. He led me from panic to pleasure. From darkness to light. From fear to faith.

Often it is in the darkness that the light of His love is discovered. Experienced. Isaiah the prophet wrote:

> In the year that king Uzziah died I saw also the Lord. . . . Then said I, . . . mine eyes have seen the King, the Lord of hosts. . . . I heard the voice of the Lord, saying, Whom shall I send, and who will go for us? Then said I, Here am I; send me. (Isa. 6:1, 5, 8)

---
[5]From the Revised Standard Version of the Bible, copyrighted 1946, 1952 © 1971, 1973.

Significantly Isaiah records the time of his transforming vision. The king had died. It was a time of loss. Void. Vacancy. Out of whatever this meant in the life of the prophet, he records that it was in a time of sorrow. The darkness of death. "In the year that king Uzziah died I saw also the Lord."

Job suffered loss and sadness. He lost his family, his wife, his wealth and his health. Yet, in the midst of his darkness he could say,

> Though He slay me, yet will I trust in him. (Job 13:15)

God honored his faith under testing, and the Bible says,

> The Lord gave Job twice as much as he had before. . . . So the Lord blessed the latter end of Job more than his beginning. (Job 42:10, 12)

In testing and in trial, in sorrow and sadness, God blesses. Out of darkness shines His light. It was "at midnight" that the apostle Paul in his jail cell prayed and sang praises to God. Suddenly an earthquake opened the doors of the prison, freeing the prisoners. And Paul ministered to them. During our midnight moments, in the midst of mourning and misery, God can move us to faith, courage and commitment.

Several of my friends have recently died. Reflecting on their lives, I scan my own. Will it make a difference that I have passed through this world? Am I living up to that to which I was born? To glorify God, enjoying Him forever! In my limited time on this planet, is the tapestry of my life conforming to the pattern God designed? His plan? It matters to Him, and it matters to me. Any impact, any influence I have, I want to be for His glory. In sharing special segments of my past, perhaps it will extend the value of my life. In lifting the lid of silence from a life that has known shock and pain, hopefully others will discover peace. Promise. Hope.

One recent evening after dinner, a friend and I waited in her beautiful garden. As dusk began to settle, we watched patiently for the lovely night-blooming primrose plant to burst forth. We waited with our eyes focused upon the plant. Confident it would open. Slowly, in its own time, one tight little bud began to unfold. Gradually, little by little as we watched, its petals spread until it became a full-blown flower. Opening only in the evening twilight, by morning it would be withered and dead.

Perhaps I, too, had blossomed in the dark night

of my divorce, discouragements and despair. The love and power of God had seemed to unfold in the darkness. He had shown me then what I would not have seen in the light. In the darkness, that far side of dawn. He had caused my faith to unfold. By the coming of dawn, as the beautiful night-blooming primrose plant had withered and died, so my selfishness and pride, pretense and vanity, deception and insincerity—all had begun the process of withering and dying. Upon my commitment to God.

Yesterday I discovered the completeness of the provision of God. Today I trust in the same God of yesterday. For tomorrow I hope. Whatever hopelessness yet cradles inside, however deep any residue of pain or cruel hurt, hope is available. Hope for here and now. Hope based on the promise of God. Promise of ultimate victory. Assurance in God's fairness, in contrast to this unfair world. Confidence that one day there will be justice. Equity. Lasting love. Peace.

Meanwhile, life continues its onward flow. In the here and the now I cope, and rise above and beyond mere managing. To conquering each crisis. Crises that ripple through the calm and the quiet that have fused on a deeper level within.

Trauma once again suddenly intruded upon the tranquility I had come to know and cherish. Sorrow once more invaded my life.

One frosty fall evening as I relaxed at home alone, a terse message broke the calm. The voice on the other end of the line informed me that my mother had just died. As prepared as I thought I was for such a moment, the shock of those words ushered in a wave of denial. It *could not be true!* I heard the words of the foreboding message, but my heart could not at that moment accept them. Feeling like an orphan, with both of my parents now gone, I did not want to accept that they were no longer living. That they were dead. And yet, had not Dwight L. Moody said,

> Some day you will read in the papers that D.L. Moody . . . is dead. Don't you believe a word of it! At that moment I shall be more alive than I am now. I shall have gone up higher, that is all; gone out of this old clay tenement into a house that is immortal, a body that death cannot touch, that sin cannot taint, a body like unto His own glorious body. I was born of the flesh in 1837. I was born of the Spirit in 1856. That which is born of the flesh may die. That which is born of the Spirit will live forever.[6]

---

[6]Paul D. Moody and A.P. Fitt, *The Shorter Life of D.L. Moody* (Chicago: The Bible Institute Colportage Association, 1900), p. 9.

I believe this. It is an integral part of my faith. And gradually the impact of the unexpected message of my mother's death began to settle. Reality gently moved in upon my thinking. Slowly, I was able to focus upon the facts. Facts as I believed them to be. Moody's faith was based on the Bible:

> So when this corruptible shall have put on incorruption, and this mortal shall have put on immortality, then shall be brought to pass the saying that is written, Death is swallowed up in victory. O death, where is thy sting? O grave, where is thy victory? (1 Cor. 15:54, 55)

I believe the words of Scripture:

> For we know that if our earthly house of this tabernacle were dissolved, we have a building of God, an house not made with hands, eternal in the heavens. (2 Cor. 5:1)

Yes, I believed! But my heart was sad. Lonely. Once more I was feeling hurt. Once again I felt heartbreak. But with a difference. The anguish at my divorce was devoid of any ray of hope. Any reason for happiness. However, my mother's death now encompassed the promise of heaven. Hope.

And therefore, healing. Any loss, any sorrow I felt, was for myself. I knew my mother was in heaven. In one of the mansions God promised He had prepared:

> In my Father's house are many mansions: if it were not so, I would have told you. I go to prepare a place for you. (John 14:2)

But we are so very human. Vulnerable. Our feelings so exposed. We know with our mind. We believe with our intellect. But our heart still grieves. It longs for the loved one. And the love that has been removed from life.

One morning I awakened deep in sorrow, my pillow wet with tears. I cried out to God, "O Lord! I cannot handle my grief. I am at the end of trying. I cannot go on. Not this way. I can't do it myself. Help me."

This new day passed as the others had, in loneliness. With a deep feeling of bereftness. Emptiness. The feelings I knew so well from those grieving days following my divorce. The familiar void in my life. The gap that now existed—again. The blank, bland sensation. The strangling malaise that made nothing feel worthy of the doing.

As evening came on, however, I remembered an incident out of my childhood.

When I was a little girl, my parents, my sister and I often drove to the home of my aunt for a visit. On the return trip my sister and I, dolls cradled in our arms, huddled beneath the warm blanket in the back seat of the old Buick. Always I fell asleep before the car pulled into the drive—home.

But, after my father parked the car in the garage, he gently lifted me in his big, strong arms, carrying me into the house. Up the stairs to my room. In the morning when I awoke, I was in my own bed. In my room.

This memory had crowded in upon my mind the day I was able to "go back home." I had noted the garage. The doorway. My bedroom. And I remembered those poignant days of childhood. Now, my heavenly Father, with His "everlasting arms," had borne my mother to her room. Up in the heavenlies. I believe it was just as gently, ever as tender as when my father carried me. Did not the apostle Paul write:

> . . . to be absent from the body, and to be present with the Lord. (2 Cor. 5:8)

Such assurance slowly moved me to an abiding peace. A sense of closure. The end of my earthly experience with my parents. A part of my life was now over. However precious it had been, it was gone. But it had prepared me to live courageously. With resiliency. Making the many grains of sand into pearls.

The strength that had surfaced grew stronger in the days following. As the weeks and months have rolled on, I look to the future—unafraid. I believe this life is a preparation for the next. A readying for a life—with God—that shall never end. I am assured of a new dawn. What I have known this side of heaven will pale as I experience what He has promised.

> Eye hath not seen, nor ear heard, neither have entered into the heart of man, the things which God hath prepared for them that love him. (1 Cor. 2:9)

Eyes have not seen! Seeing is especially precious to me. For it was high above Michigan Avenue in an office overlooking beautiful Lake Michigan that I once saw clearly for the first time. And when I saw, I wept. Sailboats were drifting lazily in the soft summer breeze. I had never before seen them far out upon the lake. Having been born with cataracts on both of my eyes, my vision had been through a blur. A foggy haze.

When a little girl, my mother brought me to an eye specialist in the city. He arranged for the photographing of my eyes at a famous Chicago hospital. Subsequent eye examinations through the years, in various cities in which I lived, corroborated what those early pictures revealed.

Amazement and fascination were consistent responses by medical men. Fellow doctors and classes of medical students studied my eyes. Echoing dismay and intrigue, they concluded with similar exclamations: "Beautiful! Intricate, delicate lacy patterns! You were born with them. You will die with them. They will never change."

However, my doctor broke the news one day in his office, as my chin was propped on the optical instrument with a high-beamed light scanning the lenses. They *had* changed. It was "one of those things."

Slowly, they grew worse. Changing gradually. At my driver's license renewal test, unable to read the letters, I struggled. Told to read line five, I silently puzzled, where *is* line five? Line four? Frenzied, I searched for line three! Obviously I was advised to see my doctor. And, confirming my fears, he set the date for surgery.

Leaving his office frightened by the unknown, I shivered in the coldness of my fear. The old familiar terror of aloneness clutched at my throat. Clawed at my heart. Palpitations pounded. I was afraid. These were the moments when loneliness and sadness rolled in like waves of the sea. Tossed between solid faith and undulating fear, my small vessel of courage felt ready to capsize. Expecting it to sink, leaving me in a sea of despair, I riveted my hope on the strength of God.

Although cataracts are common, and usually successfully removed, I believe an eye operation holds unique terror for most persons. As Helen Keller said,

> Of all the senses, I am sure that sight must be far and away the most delightful.[7]

It is this wonderful sight, whatever degree each of us has, that we are afraid of losing. For me, having been born with a film over my eyes, I had never known that my sight differed from that of others. I was not aware of the contrast that apparently existed.

Surgery on the first eye was successful. However, since my vision had worsened quite gradually, I was not prepared for the abrupt change ahead.

Now, seated in an office overlooking Lake Michigan, with perfect vision in my "new eye," I discovered those sailboats far out on the lake. I saw the skyscrapers with crystal clearness. I read the signs

---

[7] Richard Harrity and Ralph G. Martin, *Three Lives of Helen Keller* (New York: Doubleday and Company, Inc., 1962), p. 24.

down the avenue, and watched the people far below.

A year and a half later successful surgery aided the other eye. Contact lenses provided panoramic vision, opening to me a wide world of wonder. Catapulting me into a world of firsts, I stood on the brink of discovery.

After recuperation, the first Sunday I entered my church I beheld the sanctuary with a sense of awe. I now saw the exquisite detail in the magnificent stained-glass windows of this cathedral in Chicago's loop. I found, high in the nave above the choir, carvings of symbols representative of the Christian faith, enhancing the chancel. I saw clearly the depth of strength and kindness in the physical features of my pastors.

The faces of my family opened before me in expressiveness as I discovered the details of their uniqueness.

Standing beside the sea the summer following surgery, I saw the surf, surpassed in beauty only by ships silently sliding in deep waters offshore. I watched the sea gulls soar, diving in their flight of freedom.

My next visit to the mountains revealed their massiveness quite dramatically defined. Snowy peaks and slanting shoulders were outlined prominently against the sky. In the stillness and quiet solemnity I breathed a prayer of gratitude as I saw people and places clearly. Without the blur I'd known for so long. For me, later on the road of life, I had come to see clearly. To know beauty in detail.

But as glorious as my new sight has become, it does not compare with that which I shall enjoy some day. My significant sight does not prepare me for the dazzling dawn of the future. Moving away from the darkness of divorce first heralded the dawn of a new day for me. Another dawn sparkled into my life when I received new vision. Although beautiful, it is yet inadequate. Indescribable, it is still inferior.

> Now we see through a glass, darkly; but
> then face to face. (1 Cor. 13:12)

I had *always* seen "through a glass darkly." My personal experience illustrates the spiritual reality yet beyond. My preview prepares me for the promised dawn. Today is brighter because God's dawn will appear. The glass we see through now is dark. But there is more. Much more. Christ will return, one day, bringing a new dawn. Never will it end in sunset. God promised,

> And there shall be no night there, and
> they need no candle, neither light of the

sun; for the Lord God giveth them light.
(Rev. 22:5)

Perhaps until that dawn, there will always remain a residue of pain. Sorrow. Loss. There may be other dark days, but the confidence in tomorrow brings quiet. Peace. As we move from this side of dawn to His eternal dawn.

The Lord is my light and my salvation; whom shall I fear? The Lord is the strength of my life, of whom shall I be afraid?
(Ps. 27:1)

Bibliography

Augsburger, David. *Caring Enough to Confront.* Scottdale, Pa.: Herald Press, 1973.

Barnhouse, Donald Grey. *Epistle to the Romans.* Philadelphia: Donald Grey Barnhouse, 1954.

Carnegie, Dale. *How to Stop Worrying and Start Living.* New York: Simon and Schuster, Inc., 1948.

Claypool, John R. *Tracks of a Fellow Struggler.* Waco, Tex.: Word Books, Publisher, 1974.

Emerson, Ralph Waldo. "The American Scholar," as quoted in *Great Treasury of Western Thought,* edited by Mortimer J. Adler and Charles Van Doren, R. R. Bowker Company, New York, New York. Copyright © 1977 by Xerox Corporation.

Encyclopaedia Britannica. Chicago: Encyclopaedia Britannica, Inc., 1948.

Fromm, Erich. *Escape from Freedom.* New York: Rinehart and Co., Inc., 1941.

Green, Bob. *The Chicago Tribune.* January 3, 1979, Section 4, p. 2.

Harrity, Richard, and Martin, Ralph G. *Three Lives of Helen Keller.* New York: Doubleday and Company, Inc., 1962.

Keller, Helen. *We Bereaved.* New York: Leslie Fulenwider, Inc., 1929.

Lindbergh, Anne Morrow. *Gift from the Sea.* New York: Pantheon Books, Inc., 1955.

Maltz, Maxwell. *Creative Living for Today.* New York: Trident Press, 1967.

Marshall, Catherine. *The Prayers of Peter Marshall.* Lincoln, Virginia: Chosen Books, 1954.

Marshall, Peter. *Mr. Jones, Meet the Master.* New York: Fleming H. Revell Company, 1949, 1950.

Maugham, W. Somerset. *The Summing Up.* New York: Doubleday, Doran and Co., Inc., 1938.

Missildine, W. Hugh. *Your Inner Child of the Past.* New York: Simon & Schuster, Inc., 1963.

Moody, Paul D., and Fitt, A.P. *The Shorter Life of D.L. Moody.* Chicago: The Bible Institute Colportage Association, 1900.

Newman, Mildred, Berkowitz, Bernard. *How To Be Your Own Best Friend.* New York: Random House, Inc., 1971.

Pierce, Robert Bruce. "Believing a Thing In!" Sermon preached May 25, 1969, in the Chicago Temple. The First United Methodist Church.

Powell, John. *Why Am I Afraid to Tell You Who I Am?* Niles, Ill.: Argus Communications, 1969.

Rogers, Carl R. *On Becoming a Person.* Boston: Houghton Mifflin Co., 1961.

Sheehy, Gail. *Passages: Predictable Crises in Adult Life.* New York: E.P. Dutton, 1974, 1976.

Tournier, Paul. *Secrets.* Translated by Joe Embry. Richmond: John Knox Press, 1965.

Walker, Harold Blake. "Command the Morning." *The Chicago Tribune.*

Walker, Harold Blake. "Feeling Inferior." *Chicago Tribune Magazine.* August 27, 1978.

White, Ernest. *The Way of Release: For Souls in Conflict.* Fort Washington, Pa.: Christian Literature Crusade, 1947.

Young, Loretta as told to Helen Ferguson. *The Things I Had to Learn.* Indianapolis: The Bobbs-Merrill Co., Inc., 1961.